breaking
borders

kate isler

breaking borders

A Remarkable Story of Adventure, Family, and Career Success that Defied All Expectations

HARPERCOLLINS
LEADERSHIP

AN IMPRINT OF HARPERCOLLINS

Published by HarperCollins Leadership, an imprint of HarperCollins Focus LLC.

Any internet addresses, phone numbers, or company or product information printed in this book are offered as a resource and are not intended in any way to be or to imply an endorsement by HarperCollins Leadership, nor does HarperCollins Leadership vouch for the existence, content, or services of these sites, phone numbers, companies, or products beyond the life of this book.

ISBN 978-1-4002-2157-8 (eBook)
ISBN 978-1-4002-2156-1 (PBK)

Library of Congress Control Number: 2020951051

Printed in the United States of America
20 21 22 23 LSC 10 9 8 7 6 5 4 3 2 1

This book is dedicated to my "Council." In addition to the love and support from Doug and the boys, I am fortunate to have a group of BOLD women around me that have generously shared their feedback, insights, love, and my passion for getting this story told. My Council sisters (biological and soul) help guide me, offer input, a hand to hold when I am down, and raise their voices in celebration along with me. My Council enriches my life every day. I cherish and thank them.

Everyone needs a "Council" in their lives!

contents

contents

breaking borders

one

Five-by-Eight Trailer

AM NOT A SEATTLE NATIVE. I have a hard time determining where I am from. My father was a Holiday Inn manager; his official title was Inn Keeper. An Inn Keeper meant that he ran hotel operations from top to bottom, was on call 24/7, and required the Inn Keeper's family to live on the property. The family consisted of my mother, my sister, and occasionally one of my half brothers. My sister and I are thirty-two months apart, whereas with my two half brothers, one is eleven years my senior and the other is thirteen years older. We were not a close family; I don't remember my older brothers around much other than summer visits. For the most part, it was my sister and me with my parents.

When my sister, Karen, and I were very young, home was a suite or a collection of adjoining rooms and a small kitchenette in the Holiday Inn property our father was running at the time. The configuration of our living space was a straight line starting with my parents' room and ending with my sister's; mine was in the middle. The inevitable result of occupying an adjoining middle room was that it became a hallway to Karen's room. My sister and I were not close, growing up. Karen played by the rules. She was interested in boys, dressing nicely, and making good grades. I had an electronic race car track on the floor of my room, preferred kickball at recess over any type of academics, and was never really clear on the need for rules. We vied for our parents' attention and fought over everything—I was always exasperated by her constant presence passing through my room on the way to hers.

For many, the description of living in a hotel suite conjures up the vision of Eloise at the Plaza in New York; this was not my experience. Our unusual living arrangement was supplemented by full access to the restaurants and housekeeping. In all cases, we lived in motel-style properties that meant the door opened to the outside, and there was at least one swimming pool. In some ways, this was a kid's dream: one or two pools at my disposal and unlimited French fries via room service. I caught the school bus each morning, standing below the iconic Holiday Inn sign.

There was a significant downside for children to living in a commercial establishment. My sister and I went to public schools and had friends, just as other kids did; however, there were few after-school play dates at "our house." Most parents had reservations about letting their children come to play at a motel. Birthday parties were always the hardest. When I was turning eight, like most kids, my birthday and Christmas were the most significant two days of the year. I started planning my birthday party weeks in advance, making a list of everyone in my class to invite, games to play, and the flavor of cake I wanted. However, when my birthday finally arrived, only one of my classmates, Amy Paul, was able to come to the party. We received several "thank you, but we don't feel comfortable having our child in a hotel dining room for a party" responses. Like most of our birthday celebrations, this one ended up being Amy, my family, and a variety of hotel staff sharing a cake quietly in the dining room before the dinner rush.

The unease that parents felt about letting their children visit a hotel for a play date was exacerbated by the fact that we moved to a new city and a new property every few years, so we were always the new family. Parents had little context or history about us and so were hesitant to let their children spend the afternoon or sleep over at a public place. In the first ten years of my life, I lived in six cities. I mastered meeting new people, adapting and adjusting to new situations, and making friends quickly early in life as a survival skill.

By the end of seventh grade, we were living in Albuquerque, and my parents were divorced. My mother announced she was getting married again. She had been introduced to Paul a few months before and was moving us to Salt Lake City to live with him and his two children. As we started the well-practiced process of packing and saying our goodbyes to friends, the nuptials fell apart. The marriage only lasted a matter of weeks, but the embarrassment was too much for my mother to recover her dignity. She was determined to move anyway, so she adjusted the destination, and we went on packing. Our new address would be Colorado Springs, where we had lived for a short period a few years before. My mother had friends she felt comfortable with, so we loaded up the moving van, and off we went.

My father continued to live in our rooms at the hotel in Albuquerque and was still very present in our lives. There was no love lost between my parents, and by all accounts, it was a messy divorce. My father was the consummate Inn Keeper: charming, engaging, with curly hair and a deep dimple in his right cheek. He had a twinkle in his eye and spoke with a southern drawl that was still prevalent twenty-plus years after he left Mississippi. Everyone loved Louis. He seemed to know everyone and make friends easily. I was too young to remember the details, but I remember my parents' relationship as tense, adversarial. On a few occasions, it erupted into physical fights.

The First Taste of Independence

I was never without as a child. I had enough food, warm clothes, and a place to live. But once we moved out of the motel, there were few frills. A single mother without a college degree, going back to work after raising children, was an awkward position from which to command a top salary. I was a "latch key kid." *Latch key* was the term used in the 1970s to describe a growing population of kids whose parents both worked outside of the home. Children arrived home from school before the end of their parents' workday, let themselves into the house, and latched the door behind them. We were the first generation of children to gain after-school independence. To me, this was neither good nor bad. It was my life, an experience I had in common with several friends. Once school was out, I would go home and do homework, review the day's gossip on the phone, and watch sitcoms on TV until dinnertime. Living in an apartment with a single mother put me squarely in the ordinary category among kids at the time. The "latch key" status was my first taste of independence and self-reliance, and it felt great.

My independent streak continued in high school. I was young for my class, with a late September birthday, and entered high school as a sophomore at fourteen. The legal driving age was sixteen in Colorado. The result was that I was dependent on friends and my sister for transportation until my junior year. It was under these conditions that I had my first job other than babysitting. My sister worked a few evenings a week and on the weekend as a hostess at a local hotel restaurant. Having grown up in the hotel business, playing behind the front desk and eating in the hotel restaurant for most meals, this was a familiar environment for both of us. I was hired at the same hotel restaurant as "busgirl." This prestigious position required a uniform consisting of L'eggs suntan pantyhose, ugly orthopedic-looking white shoes, a black skirt just below my knees, white shirt, and ill-fitting gold vest. As a teenager, this was not a look you wanted your friends to see. I was too young to be hired, but my sister put in a good word, and the manager knew my father. Having extra cash in high school for investment into fast food and contributions to the weekend keg parties was essential.

Because I was reliant on my sister, Karen, for transportation, our shifts were scheduled at the same time, including working the buffet on Sundays that started at 6:00 a.m. Working the same shifts also meant that my sister, the hostess, was my direct supervisor. Karen had always been the rule follower, which extended directly from the bossy old sister role to the supervisor at Palmer House dining room. I never cleared tables of dirty dishes fast enough, never delivered water and bread at the right time, and always needed to comb my hair, all of which she reminded me of constantly.

Karen was a senior and the toast of the school. She was head cheerleader, on student government, and always dated the most popular athlete of the season. We couldn't have been more different. I chose to befriend the misfits. My friends were not the kids that got into big trouble; they were more the kids that sat just outside of the cool kids' social circle but were also friendly with the "heads," the nickname given to the real troublemakers. The "heads" were the kids who smoked, skipped classes regularly, and were in after-school detention so often they had assigned seats. Some of my friends were siblings of kids in the "in-group" my sister ran with, but most were just awkward teenagers trying to figure out where they fit in among the thousand students in the public school we attended.

I endured the humiliation of my sister bossing me around in all aspects of my life before taking the first opportunity that came up to move to the hotel's front desk. During my long hours of clearing dirty dishes from tables and running odd errands for the servers and kitchen staff, I had earned a reputation for working hard and being pleasant and articulate to customers. When a customer would complain about their meal, I would leverage my Inn Keeper's daughter training and would offer an immediate apology and have the food remade or taken off the bill. This quick resolution without having to escalate cemented my good reputation, and when the position of switchboard operator on the afternoon shift from 3:00 p.m. to 11:00 p.m. came up, I was a shoo-in. Transportation became the biggest challenge of my new job. I managed with my bike and the help of my friends who were older and had cars.

As with most teenagers, the summer between my sophomore and junior years in high school was all about friends. I was sure that I knew everything there was to know about life, and my parents couldn't possibly understand what it was like to be young. My single mother was preoccupied with her job and a new boyfriend, my sister was off to college, and I was working and socializing. Much of the time, I was left on my own to navigate daily life.

School started in September, and my birthday was a few weeks later. This was a big one, sixteen. I could finally get my driver's license. I had saved most of my paychecks and had just enough money to buy a used car. My mother had been married and divorced for a third time and now was living most of the time with a man who had a passion for refurbishing older cars. I looked in the newspaper classified ads and found a Ford Mustang that I could afford, so I took my mother's boyfriend to check it out. The car was not the cool Mustang from the movies. Instead, it was the boxy baby blue compact version from the early seventies. I bought it. The one setback was that I still didn't have a driver's license. So, there we were, in my brand-new-to-me car, and my mother's boyfriend was the first to drive it.

I knew how to drive from spending summers with my father. Soon after my mother moved us to Colorado, my father left his job at the Holiday Inn and took a position running the guest operations for a large ranch in northern New Mexico. All the roads on the ranch were dirt, so I learned to drive a stick-shift pickup truck at fourteen.

I had passed the driver's ed class offered at school, and I owned a car. The only thing left was to take the driving test.

On my sixteenth birthday, a friend took me home during the lunch period. I got in my car and drove to the department of licensing. It was early afternoon; the line was short, and I breezed through the practical test without any problem.

The examiner in the passenger seat signed my license in official ink, congratulated me, and told me I could get my parents and leave. I must have looked guilty because as soon as he handed off the two-and-a-quarter-by-three-inch card that gave me the independence

I was craving, he frowned and asked which of my parents had accompanied me to the licensing office. I panicked inside. Dad lived three hours away, and Mom was not available.

My emotions were high, I was ready for true independence, and it was right there. Every moment without that little card was a moment that I was stuck bumming rides or riding my bike, and I knew I would do anything that I had to in order for him to hand over my license. Fortunately, the examiner had a heart. He didn't look happy but thankfully let it slide with a stern warning that, if he had known, he would never have passed me. He got out of the car, shaking his head, and I drove away relieved that the examiner was understanding and thrilled with my new legal independence.

Having a driver's license was the key to unlocking several areas of my life. And my quest to get that license taught me that convention was a wall that could be climbed. I knew that I had to get to the testing center and wasn't about to wait around until it was convenient for one of my parents to take me. This was the first time I remember moving forward to achieve a goal without worrying too much that my approach wasn't ordinary. No one had ever come right out and said that I couldn't drive myself, so I just did. That was my intro to living life in the gray area.

Off and Running

Driving opened an entirely new world for me. I left the hotel switchboard and started working at a fast-food chain (as is required for every teenager at one time or another). I was going to school but was bored to death. My grades were passing, but not great, and I continued to run with the fringe crowd. My friend Kim had an older brother who was working at a new high-tech production plant close to our neighborhood and told me about openings for part-time employees. The job was swing shift, 2:00 p.m. to 8:00 p.m., paid three times the hourly rate of any fast-food chain plus overtime to assemble cables on a production line for Digital Equipment Company. I was sixteen, and at least five years younger than all of my coworkers. The industrial work environment with older coworkers shifted my focus away from high school and my teenage peers. I already enjoyed a tremendous amount of freedom living with a single mother who worked full-time, and now that I was earning a sizable salary, I was self-sufficient and making the most of it. While not in trouble, I was undoubtedly brushing the edge of it, passing all my classes at school but in no way reaching my potential.

My father came to visit at Christmas and suggested that more oversight of my life was in order. I loved his life on the ranch, but the nearest town was forty miles away on a dirt road and not practical for me to attend school. The next option was to move in with my aunt and uncle in Mississippi. I had always loved visiting them and felt at home with their lifestyle and family. They had three of seven children still at home, so one more didn't faze them. I moved during Christmas break and began the second semester of my junior year at Heritage Upper School in northeastern Mississippi. Back in Colorado, my class size was over four hundred, so it was a culture shock to find out that there were only forty-three students in the junior class, and everyone knew everyone and everything that was happening with the upper school students. The semester I spent in Mississippi was one of the most formative times of my life. I went from having no one to answer to and the run of the house, to having adults that were very present, living in a small community that was always alert and watching, and three teenage boys in the house and at school to contend with. I loved it! I worked afternoons at my aunt's gift shop and was instantly popular as the new girl in a small school. For the first time, I had a curfew, required homework, and built-in brothers to fight with and confide in. I learned how to study, sneak in and out of the house with adults home, and what it was like to have a close family.

By the start of my senior year, I was ready to move forward, and the idea of another year at a small-town school was too confining. I returned to Colorado and attended an alternative project-based program to finish my remaining high school credits. One of my classmates was Erika, a girl from Seattle, Washington. Erika was unlike anyone I had ever met. She had an air of sophistication, even at seventeen. She read poetry and smoked Marlboro Red cigarettes and had the same birthday as I did. I was in awe of Erika from the first time I met her. We became friends and kept in touch when she went back to Seattle. I visited her in Seattle for a week following high school graduation, which had only deepened my admiration and envy of her life. She lived just north of downtown on Queen Anne Hill in a big old house on a tree-lined street. Her friends drank beer, played in bands, listened to eclectic music, and had the run of the city. Being there left an impression. I realized that I loved city life.

I arrived at Colorado Mountain College as a seventeen-year-old freshman. I loved the small mountain school surrounded by some of the best ski areas in the Rockies. I studied photography, skied whenever possible, and got a job working at the Hot Spring Pool, the city's main attraction. My gym classes freshman year were kayaking and whitewater rafting, and I found my passion. I wanted to spend all my time on the river. Glenwood Springs was a small community, and through my whitewater gym class, I met a river guide from a local rafting company. I took the short instructor's course and signed on as a guide as soon as I was qualified.

My job as a river guide was to entertain eight to ten people on a three-and-a-half-hour boat trip down the upper Colorado River. I was responsible for getting the boat from the drop-off point down the river to a pullout where the bus would be waiting with coolers of beer and soft drinks. During the trip, I relayed stories about historic places along the river, made up legends about creatures roaming the banks, and told jokes from the back of a fourteen-foot rubber paddleboat.

It was an ideal life. I rafted all day, drank beer all evening, and moved into a house with two boys and one girl. All of us were river guides.

That summer, I met my first love, Mack. He was from Denver and attended the University of Northern Colorado (UNC). He came to Glenwood to live with friends and work as a river guide for the season. We quickly became inseparable. He decided to stay in Glenwood for the winter while I finished my AA program, then we would move to Greeley and attend UNC together.

That winter, Mack; another river guide friend, "Red"; and I started to talk about how much money we could make if we owned our own rafting business rather than guiding for someone else. Alpine Adventures was born.

Blue Sky Rafting was the top company in town, so we agreed that our company name had to start with an "A," so it would be the first rafting company in the paper phone book's alphabetical listing of businesses. We pooled the money we had made during the winter as capital and bought three used rafts and an old school bus. We passed out flyers advertising full and half-day raft trips to tourists in town and around the Hot Springs pool. We rented a small office and had a phone line installed to take reservations. We could not afford office furniture, so we spent a lot of time sitting on the floor, playing cards, and waiting for the rush of tourists to come through the door. There were many down days, but we made it work and earned enough for rent, food, and beer with a little extra to go toward tuition the coming year. It was a fantastic experience and my first business venture.

Redefining My Vision

I graduated from Colorado Mountain College (CMC) with an associate degree and transferred to the University of Northern Colorado (UNC) as a junior. The plan was that Mack and I would both finish school at UNC and live happily ever after. At nineteen years old, things don't always go as planned.

We shut Alpine Adventures down at the end of August. My father called and said he was short of serving staff at the ranch and asked if I would come for a working visit before starting school. I always loved time at the ranch, and the additional money would be welcome for school expenses. The opportunity seemed like a windfall.

After a few weeks working at the ranch, I headed for Greeley to begin moving into a basement apartment we had rented close to campus. Mack was stopping by his parents' house for a few days in Denver before coming up to get settled before classes began.

Moving day was the day I found out that, while I was away, Mack had found another Kate to replace me. Yep, her name was the same as mine, and I knew her well. She was a friend that ran in the same crowd, and Mack had worked for her father on a construction crew during the winter. I was devastated; this was my first real love and the man that I had built a vision of my life around.

I had enrolled at UNC and moved to Greeley to maintain my relationship with Mack and had never even considered going to school anywhere else. I was self-reliant and mature in many ways but so completely naïve in others. I had built my life plan assuming that this was going to be my husband.

The news that Mack had been unfaithful was delivered by the wife of a mutual friend from our social circle in Glenwood Springs. The couple was a few years older than most of my friends and had moved from Glenwood Springs to Greeley the year before. They had married early in college and now had a newborn baby. We all looked up to them and admired the life that they were building. It was the model for the life I thought I wanted.

It was during that tough conversation on the curb outside of my dingy basement apartment in Greeley that I knew for sure that I didn't want the life I saw playing out in front of me. I had options and the opportunity to make choices that would impact my adult life. I could forgive him, pretend that it didn't happen and that I didn't mind an occasional stray. This was the counsel of almost all our well-meaning friends. Times were different then. The idea of finding your husband at nineteen was not strange, and many couples were willing to overlook certain indiscretions to make the relationship work. I was not one of them. Several of us were moving to Greeley and nearby Fort Collins to finish our four-year degrees, and a rift like this could have a significant impact on our friend group. Or I could stand up for myself.

I had learned from my parents' many failed relationships that I couldn't settle for this. I felt betrayed, not only by Mack but also because several of our friends were aware of this incident and didn't tell me. I felt as though our friends had chosen him over me; they encouraged me to move on and get over it. I felt completely abandoned but also resolute. I was not going to ever feel this way again. Mack never moved to Greeley.

Classes started, I met new people, and began a new life of my own making. I slowly drifted away from the friend group that came from Glenwood Springs. I was busy with classes, a job, and meeting new people that were relevant to the life I was living without Mack. It was hard to lose close friendships that had started as we entered adulthood. I still think about those people and that time of my life fondly. We were growing up and learning lessons about adulthood daily. It was painful to lose that, but the choice was clear.

There was one notable dissenter in the Glenwood group of advisors: Carrie. Carrie stuck by my side and is one of my dearest friends to this day. Carrie's parents lived on the "western slope" of the Rockies about fourteen miles west of Greeley in Loveland, Colorado. She had been a year ahead of me at Colorado Mountain College and ran in the same circle. She was going to school at UNC and living with her parents in Loveland. It wasn't long before she became my de facto roommate. Carrie and I went to class, studied till all hours, endured dating drama, went to parties, drank beer, and worked at part-time jobs. At the end of the spring quarter, Carrie announced that she was going to backpack in Europe in July and August. Traveling to Europe was something that I couldn't imagine, much less afford, even though I wanted to see the world very much at that time. I knew I would miss her daily companionship but wished her well and agreed to look for a better apartment while she was away.

It was late August, Carrie would be home from Europe soon, and finals for summer classes were in full swing. The lease on my apartment would be up soon, and I was at a decision point. I was an average student and had started at UNC as an elementary education major. After a two-week student teaching trial run, it was clear that

I was not cut out to spend all day molding young minds. Teaching was not my calling. Life in Greeley was fun, but I was having second thoughts about staying for another year. I was restless and needed an adventure. My whole life, I had moved around with my parents and gone to schools that allowed me to have experiences—the alternative high school, starting my own business, and following Mack and my friends to Greeley. I wanted something more exciting, something more meaningful, and something more daring. Why not move to Seattle? I loved the time I had spent there following high school. I had an associate's degree plus a year of college coursework completed. I was willing to work hard and determined to succeed. There was no reason not to give it a shot.

With my mind made up, I contacted my friend Erika, shared my plans to move, and asked to stay with her at her parents' house for a few weeks while I found an apartment. I decided that I needed to finish school when I got to Seattle, so I investigated universities in the area and found that I needed to save money and become a Washington State resident before continuing with school. It was a trade-off I was willing to make.

Word of my plans spread quickly through the old CMC friend community. The group was now dispersed from Denver north across three major college towns on the western slope of Colorado, but news of this magnitude travels fast. I couldn't wait for Carrie to return home so I could tell her my plan. I would leave Colorado to take up residence in Seattle the week after she returned from Europe. I was hoping she would understand and support my decision to leave the relative security of Greeley and come along, at least for the drive to Seattle.

I was counting the days until I was on the road to the Pacific Northwest and my big adventure. I was in the library with my head buried in a textbook when I felt someone join me at the table. I looked up and was shocked to see Mack pulling up a chair across from me. I hadn't seen him for months and was surprised and puzzled with the encounter. I stiffened my spine and asked what he was doing in town and, more importantly, in the library sitting at my study table.

There was little small talk, as he was nervous, looking down, fidgeting with his hands. He had come to tell me that he was getting married to a woman he had been dating in Denver. I wasn't surprised as they had dated for several months, and by all reports, things were getting serious. I was sad on one level, as he was my first real love, but I had moved on and was now about to embark on an entirely new life, and I wasn't sure what he was doing there.

The real surprise came when he explained why he had come to deliver the news of his engagement in person. He had heard that I was moving to Washington, and he was now having second thoughts about getting married. He asked if we could take another shot at our relationship and said that if I didn't move, he wouldn't get married. I was speechless. Mack had always been arrogant, but this was stunning even from him! He cheated on me with a friend, was engaged to a different woman, and now was professing his love for me. If I gave in to him, I knew I would never fully trust him, and our relationship would be a series of betrayals. That was the moment I knew for sure I was doing the right thing. I couldn't imagine how hurt and sad his fiancée would be that he was having this conversation. I wondered if she knew what kind of guy he really was.

Mack had broken my heart with this type of behavior a year ago. I looked him straight in the eye as calmly as I could and suggested he have an honest discussion with his fiancée about his feelings and wished him the best for the rest of his life. I slammed my book closed and walked away, turning my attention to the move to Seattle. That was the last time I ever saw Mack. I have no idea if he married or not.

A few days later, I picked Carrie up from the airport and shared my plans. I can remember sitting in the car and my heart beating because I wasn't sure how she would take it. We were supposed to room together, and she had a right to be frustrated. But I worried for nothing. She quickly agreed to drive with me to Seattle. She wasn't ready to leave Colorado herself but understood and supported my need for adventure and change.

I packed up the necessities from the basement apartment, rented a five-by-eight U-Haul trailer, and early one morning, three weeks before I turned twenty-one, with the music blaring, Carrie, my cat Griz, and I headed north on I-25 out of Greeley and out of Colorado. Seattle or Bust!

The heady feeling of adventure and independence came to a halt when we realized that we could move forward with the trailer hitched to the car but had no idea how to back up. We tried everything to figure it out. We even asked someone who said . . . no luck. This wasn't going to stop us. We would just have to focus on the road ahead.

After two and a half days of moving forward, by necessity, we drove into Seattle. It was midafternoon and long before mobile phones and Google Maps, so we immediately got hopelessly lost looking for Erika's parents' house on the hill. It was the first taste of the city with a restless cat and our forward-facing trailer, but we had made it.

Carrie and I spent the next few days looking for apartments and learning areas of the city based on listings in the newspaper classified ads. I quickly found work at a one-hour-film shop in the University District and an apartment close by in the Capitol Hill neighborhood. Both areas were filled with young people, not yet gentrified, so still very affordable.

The apartment had been built during the Seattle expansion for the World's Fair in 1962. It was a budget, mid-century building with two security doors and nine one- and two-bedroom units perched on a steep section of a busy street that served as the main artery from downtown to the Capitol Hill neighborhood. My unit was on the second floor, northeast corner, overlooking the section of the street just where cars shifted to get up the last bit of the hill. It was a one-bedroom with large corner windows, a small bathroom and bedroom, and a dark wooden built-in bookshelf separating the tiny kitchen from a living room. The building was in a great location, with access to buses and shops just off the neighborhood high street. The only drawback was there were no pets allowed, so I didn't mention the cat on the rental application and signed a one-year lease.

Carrie and I unloaded the trailer, bought a can of white paint for the bookshelves, and within a few hours had moved the contents of my life, including the smuggled cat, into the apartment. Not being long on patience, we painted the bookshelves and unpacked the books the same night. Only later would I realize that our impatience had resulted in the books becoming a permanent part of the newly white bookshelf. A few additional hours of drying would have made all the difference. We had a good laugh and shared a six-pack of beer to celebrate my new home. Carrie flew home to Colorado the next morning, and I was truly on my own.

Lessons

1. Make friends fast. There are always people you relate to immediately. Why wait to make friends?

2. You are capable of way more than you think you are. Look within yourself for strength.

3. Taking risks pays off. I learned a ton and had a ton of fun as a first-time business owner. I didn't make millions, but made enough to live through the summer and pay for part of school the following year. Incremental lessons and wins are worth the risk.

4. Be honest with yourself about what you are willing to live with and stick to it no matter how hard it seems in the moment.

5. Create a vision for what you want your life to be and live it. I took a chance to create the life I pictured myself living and made it happen.

two

Seattle or Bust

STARTED A JOB AT A retail film development shop on University Avenue a few weeks after arriving in Seattle, ten days before my twenty-first birthday. I secured the cat in the bathroom each morning and took the bus to work. Life felt very urban, exciting, and new.

The work at the film store was the same type of part-time job I had done in Greeley. Fast film-processing shops were popping up everywhere, usually with the same photo processing equipment. They provided an easy job as the store manager.

The University District was a busy neighborhood with a young population and a great place to find my feet in the city. Money was tight, so I took my lunch to work and fixed a dinner of Rice-A-Roni mixed with frozen vegetables on most days.

My twenty-first birthday came and went without much fanfare. I had been independent for some time, and my friends had always been older and happily supplied alcohol, so the traditional twenty-first birthday night out was not that appealing. I was new to the city and had started to meet a few people, most of whom were friends of Erika's. Our birthdays were the same day, so I tagged along for her celebration on an actual night I was able to drink legally.

Don't You Have Keys for This Car?

A few days after my birthday, late in the afternoon, a guy came to the shop to drop off two rolls of film; one was a regular print film and the other slides. I followed the usual procedure of taking the film canisters as I filled out the paperwork and explaining that his prints would be ready for pickup in an hour, but the slides needed different processing, which would take three to five business days. He had a friendly tone with a smile that engulfed his entire face. But with this news, he made it clear he was not happy about waiting for the slides. He questioned me about a one-hour-film store not having the ability to process film within the one hour promoted in the name.

Clearly fishing for something to keep the conversation going, he playfully challenged me about how private the print images I prepared in the store were. This store, like most of the express photo labs at the time, had a large front window that clearly showed prints coming out of the processing machine on an assembly line that could be viewed by anyone standing on the street looking in the window. Seeing the photos coming out was an attraction. People loved to see what types of photos were coming out, and it was very rare to get anything racy at these quick processing labs. My inquisitive customer quickly moved on to other inquiries about the process, the store, and Seattle as a whole. I answered what I could but needed to help the other customers that had come into the tiny storefront. He was pleasant and seemed to be enjoying taking up my time. It was clear he was flirting, and I enjoyed the attention. The day ended, I took the bus home, and I thought nothing more about it.

The next morning, I was working in the back of the store when the bell on the front door began to ring. The store opened at 10:00 a.m. There was a supply of envelopes and a drop box next to the door for customers to leave film for processing outside of business hours. The bell kept ringing, and the door started to rattle. When I got to the counter, I found the guy with the slides and all the questions from the previous afternoon standing outside. I shook my head "no" and pointed to the drop box and instructions about film drop-off and turned back to the task of setting up for the day. He tried the door again and rang the bell, still wearing that ridiculous smile on his face. Our conversation the day before was friendly and fun. I couldn't help but like him.

I relented and opened the door to collect his film and send him on his way. With the door cracked, he broke into a lengthy explanation about the contents of his photos from the fishing boats in Alaska and how precious they were, and he didn't feel comfortable leaving them outside in the box. He pleaded to come in to hand off the film to me so that he knew it would be safe and in good hands. I could tell that he was again making up excuses to continue our conversation. He had the same friendly tone as the day before and seemed completely harmless, so I let him the rest of the way in the door. It was apparent he was flirting, and honestly, I was lonely and needed a bit of attention. He had a mop of curly blond hair and huge blue eyes with an ornery twinkle. His name was Doug.

We got the film paperwork out of the way, and he flashed me that huge smile and asked if I had plans for the evening. I had been twenty-one for less than a week and knew very few people in the area. I didn't have plans that night or any night. He asked what time I would be finished with work and told me he would be back as he strolled out the door. Meeting men and dating had always been a challenge for me. At this time, the options were limited to meeting someone at work or a bar. Neither seemed likely in my situation. The university district was full of young people, mostly students, so meeting a customer and going on a date was a great way to build a social network, and it felt much less seedy than giving my number to a guy at a bar.

It was hard to concentrate on work that day. But it was Friday, and the store was busy, so luckily, time passed quickly. At the end of the day, as I was cleaning up the store, I looked up just in time to see Doug walk, or more accurately, bounce, in the front door. He had been shopping and was wearing all new clothes. In the days before "pre-washed denim," new jeans were like stiff cardboard and colored with a very dark-blue dye that came off on your hands when you touched them. Doug was wearing a brand-new pair of cardboard jeans, a new shirt that had never come close to an iron, and clean, very bright new sports shoes. It made me giggle, but it was Friday night, the first Friday night that I could go out and legally have a drink in a bar, so I was all in. I locked the front door, and we headed down the street.

Because I was new to the area and took the bus to work, I was not familiar with much of the city. This date seemed like a great way to broaden my horizons and see more of Seattle. Besides, I was broke, and the idea of a cute guy taking me out to dinner rather than Rice-A-Roni in my apartment with the cat was appealing.

We rounded the corner about a block from the film store and approached a small brown car. He opened the passenger door for me, and I climbed in. He went around to the driver's side, slid in, and immediately leaned down and started fooling with the wires under the dashboard. When I asked what he was doing, he responded, "Starting the car." As we drove away, I looked in the ignition, and there were no keys. He maneuvered the car into traffic, and we headed west toward the waterfront neighborhood of Ballard.

My mind was racing. There was something about this guy that I really liked and I immediately felt at ease and comfortable with him. Running through the encounters we'd had in the past forty-eight hours, Doug was endearing, warm, and clearly had an air of fun about him. He was unlike anyone I had met or dated. During the drive, I had a few fleeting worries that I shouldn't be in a car with a man that I didn't know and who it was clear didn't own the vehicle. I reassured myself that I did have some information about him—a phone number captured on a film envelope—so how bad could he be?

I finally got the nerve to ask about the keys. He explained that he had been working for the National Marine Fisheries Service in Alaska and that his visits to Seattle were only for a few days on either side of his trips north, so it did not make sense to rent a place. Instead, he stayed at the YMCA, or with other fisheries employees that lived locally doing the same types of jobs in the Bering Sea. In this case, he was staying at a coworker's house, and the guy had neglected to leave the keys before heading to Alaska. I did mention the fact that if the guy hadn't left his keys, it might have been an indication that he didn't want the car used. Doug listened to my observation as he drove on and gave a slight shake of his head as an acknowledgment that he heard but didn't add anything more to his original explanation. Doug had spent his childhood in Pittsburgh, where he'd acquired several useful life skills; hot-wiring cars was only the first of many that would come to light over the years.

The first date was wonderful. Doug told me fantastic tales of growing up in an inner-city working-class neighborhood with four siblings, working on riverboats to save money for college, and about fishing boats in Alaska with all-foreign crews. He introduced me to food and drinks I had never even heard of. Best of all, he made me laugh. At the end of the night, he took me back to my apartment, and we agreed to go sightseeing in Seattle the following Sunday. It was magic. He was charming, fun, had a big heart, and we had endless things to talk about.

Autumn in Seattle can be spectacular, warm, and bright with mountains and water everywhere you look. That Sunday was a perfect day to explore the city. My transient guide and I started our adventure at Pike Place Market. He provided explanations of all the fish on display; we visited popular watering holes and ended up at the Space Needle. During the afternoon, we had talked about how close Seattle was to Canada and about how neither of us had ever been out of the country. During the day, I had fallen in love with my new hometown and had a crush on my tour guide. We exchanged phone numbers at the end of the evening. I was sad, but our lives were headed in entirely different directions, so we said our goodbyes.

The weekend had been just what I needed to start to feel at home in my new city. The adventure had taken me to new areas and given me an easy entrance to legal adulthood. Monday was a terrible day on all accounts. Nothing at the photo shop went right. None of my coworkers showed up to work, and the shop owner was less than sympathetic. I was making minimum wage and not at all thrilled with the prospects of a career as a retail photo lab manager. I had nothing to lose, so, at the end of the day, I walked out, locked the door, and decided never to return to the one-hour photo lab. On the bus home, I decided as long as I was gambling, I would call Doug and see if he had left town and if he was interested in taking a trip across the border to Vancouver with me. With shaky hands, I dialed the number. At 8:00 a.m. the next morning, we were in my car headed north on I-5, determined to leave the USA for the first time in our lives. We had no idea that a simple trip to Vancouver would be the beginning of hundreds of trips to foreign nations that we would take together.

We hit all the tourist hot spots in Vancouver and had a ball. We laughed, talked, and got to know each other for two days, but our time in Canada came to an end quickly. He had a flight to catch, and I needed to find a new job to continue to build my life in Seattle. I liked him but considered the whole episode a crazy adventure and knew it was time to get on with being responsible.

Quit! Or I Will Have to Fire You

My friend Erika had been working as a receptionist in the corporate offices of a local sportswear company. She was getting a promotion and asked if I would be interested in taking her position. It seemed easy enough: answer the phones, take messages, greet visitors, and occasionally do light office administration projects. The pay was much better than retail. Within a week of returning from Canada, I started my first office job. I was excited about the stability that an office job seemed to offer and felt very adult. The hours were predictable, and I was no longer dealing with customers off the street. I had no experience with office workers, what they really did, or what to expect. My father always had an office off the lobby of the hotel, but his job was to engage with guests. I didn't really know what office workers did all day, but this job seemed like a step up in every way.

The reception desk was on the fourth floor, surrounded by the executive offices of Generra Sportswear. I have always been a keen student of people. From a very young age, I had exposure to all types of people at the motel, but this was different. From my vantage point in the center of the top floor of the building, I was surrounded by the key leaders of the company, five days a week, eight hours a day. There was little in the way of foot traffic from visitors, which left time to observe these executives.

Being a receptionist is somewhat like being an appliance. People knew I was there and counted on my work, but most of the time, I was invisible. I saw how the leaders treated their staff, treated one another, and how they got things done (or not). I was not aware of it at the time, but my experience at Generra was a foundational training for my executive life.

The executive lineup included the CEO and his wife, the COO, the vice president of merchandising, and the president. The CEO, his wife, and their team were the designers at the company. To me, they had exotic and fascinating lives. They created all the clothing designs, had meetings, and often traveled to amazing international destinations. The president oversaw running the business, distribution, and sales teams. He was a tyrant! He yelled about everything, stomped in and out of meetings, and *never* smiled or stopped to say hello. The COO was quiet, friendly, a family man whose wife and kids visited regularly. His staff loved him and worked hard to deliver for him.

The VP of merchandising was a woman: my first woman executive role model. Marianne was very different than her male colleagues. She was deliberate, calm, and driven. She was pleasant to her team and always seemed to have the upper hand with things around the fourth floor. People at the company were immediately drawn to her and showed up outside her office door, hoping for a minute to talk almost every day.

Generra Sportswear is also where I met my soul sister and dearest friend: my boss, Barbara (Barb). She worked in the computer room, back in the day when computers worked on tapes in a cooled, clean room, and she had responsibility for the reception staff. There were two shifts for the receptionist; the day shift was from 7:00 a.m. to 4:00 p.m., and the night shift was 4:00 p.m. to 7:00 p.m. Most of the fashion buyers were on the East Coast, so it was vital to have someone handling the phones early in the morning. Manufacturing was in Asia, so it was convenient to have calls answered later in the evening. I was on the day shift and settled into my new routine and bus route. The office was quiet early in the morning, and I had started night classes, so I used the time for homework, catching up on magazines, and doing my nails before nine a.m.

There were two drawbacks to my office job. First, I was bored to death once I mastered the executives' preferences—e.g., when to stay out of the president's way and not to put calls from his ex-wife through for *any* reason, and how each of the salespeople liked their messages and visitors managed, like when to deliver the "I'm so sorry, but [Name] is not available" in the most convincing voice possible while they were standing in front of me. Second, I was a prisoner to my post. I couldn't leave the desk unless the building was on fire. I had to plan to use the bathroom when someone was available to cover the phone. Truth be told, I was terrible at office work; my typing was slow, and I would much rather be reading magazines or doing my nails than welcoming people to the office.

My receptionist career at Generra lasted close to a year. By that time, I was going nuts and knew that my future was not in office administration. Around that time, Generra was purchased by a more well-known clothing manufacturing company in the southern United States, and things were changing around the office. Barb and I had become close friends and often went to lunch together. She was planning her wedding and began using the midday break to shop for wedding things. I went along to provide my opinion. One lunch hour, as Barb and I were walking down the street to a sandwich shop we frequented, she got serious and said she had something to tell me. Her message was short and to the point. She told me that I needed to quit my job before she had to fire me. I was shocked and relieved all at once. She said that I was terrible at being a receptionist and "not customer service oriented." It was clear to her early on that my life's work would not be as a receptionist. We laugh now, knowing that it was hard for her to deliver the message, but it was such a relief for me to hear. I was over answering the phones, greeting visitors, and waiting on executives.

Even then, I knew that I was determined to be a decision-maker and business leader. Having a front-row view into the working style of the Generra executive team was a window into my future. The stereotypes were all on that team, and I saw how customers, employees, and business partners reacted to them. In the early years of my career, I reflected on them and leveraged the lessons I learned from the behavior I witnessed in a variety of situations.

I held a series of odd jobs for a year and a half after leaving Generra and attended classes at Seattle Pacific University. I couldn't afford to be a full-time student, but managed to secure market research projects that allowed me to work independently around my class schedule. I also got another weekend photo lab job and filled in on a friend's housecleaning crew when possible. I moved to a smaller apartment in a less desirable neighborhood and went back to eating Rice-A-Roni to save money. I was still managing to pay the bills and getting increasingly comfortable with Seattle.

I continued dating Doug during this time. He was still working in Alaska, so we didn't see each other face-to-face often, but there had been an instant connection between us. Both of us wanted to see where it would go. He moved from working for National Marine Fisheries, a government agency, to a private company that supplied American representatives onboard foreign vessels fishing in US waters to ensure that fishing rules were being followed. In effect, he went from the science of fisheries to the commerce of fisheries. He had many friends and contacts in the business, so the transition was smooth, and it doubled his salary.

After a few fishing seasons (a season typically lasted for the two or three months when people were allowed to catch a particular fish species) onboard foreign processing vessels, he was offered a position at a land-based fish-processing plant in Dutch Harbor, Alaska. There is no question that there were upsides to him taking a land-based job; mainly, it was much safer. In his time working at sea, he was on "catcher boats," which were converted crab boats that dragged the Bering Sea for cod and pollock for delivery to processing ships. They often iced up and several rolled over and sunk in the stormy northern seas.

Second, having him on land afforded us more regular contact. While at sea, the catcher boats and other fleet representatives acted as mail carriers. This mail carrier service ended up being a sporadic and sometimes chaotic form of communication. You never knew when you would receive a phone call from someone coming to shore tasked with delivering letters from Doug or collecting letters to take to him. Often, a call would come with an offer to transport mail if I could be at the dock for the handoff within a few hours. To adapt to this crazy message exchange, we begin writing journal-type letters and adding a bit each day so that correspondence could be ready at a moment's notice.

Our letters were complemented by an occasional middle-of-the-night HAM radio call. HAM radio contact was a complicated and very public form of communication. It involved having just the right conditions on the fishing grounds, the right weather, the time between fish deliveries, the correct range, and willing mainland-based operators to manage the call. When the stars aligned, I would be woken, most often in the middle of the night, by the phone ringing and someone announcing that they had Doug Isler on the phone, was I able to talk? Once I agreed, they would instruct me that this was a radio call and that when I finished with my side of a conversation, I needed to say "over" and wait for a response. They would also remind me that anyone on that radio channel could also hear the conversation. This meant *everyone* in the Bering Sea had a front-row seat to our long-distance relationship. Not to mention that using radio etiquette is essential, even though it is a bit unnerving to say "over" several times in a conversation when talking with a boyfriend that you liked and desperately missed. Neither of us dared the very public declaration of " I love you, *over*."

> **Neither of us dared the very public declaration of "I love you, *over*."**

All this unnatural communication allowed Doug and me time and space to get to know each other and to share our thoughts and dreams in a more profound way than would have been possible with the luxury of seeing each other regularly. The result was a much stronger bond and a mingling of our souls.

I had now been in Seattle for almost two years and was approaching the end of the spring quarter at Seattle Pacific University (SPU). I had twelve credits to go and was planning on taking classes during the summer session so that I could participate in graduation ceremonies.

Doug was in Alaska working at the shore-based processing plant, and we agreed that my graduation present would be to go for a visit to Dutch Harbor and get a taste of his life in Alaska. A few days after the graduation ceremony, and before summer classes started, I boarded a flight to Dutch Harbor via Anchorage. It was the last week of June, and as we circled for a landing on the tiny airstrip in Dutch Harbor I could see snow on the waterline. *Yikes*.

I stayed in Dutch Harbor for a total of three weeks, which is nineteen days longer than anyone else stayed there. Back then, Dutch Harbor was a small stopping point on the way in or out of the Bering Sea. It was an odd little place that only existed to service the fishing industry. The town consisted of one store that stocked everything from food to fabric to fishing licenses and just about anything you would need or want to spend several weeks on a boat in the far reaches of the northern fishing grounds. Fresh produce and dairy arrived once a week, and it was like Black Friday at Walmart to get lettuce and milk: an all-out scramble to the dairy case. There was a hotel, one restaurant, and one bustling bar.

My time in Dutch Harbor was an explicit declaration of love, and during my stay, we spent time talking about the rest of our lives together. While I loved him, it was apparent to me that our life together was not going to be as Dutch Harbor residents. But I knew that I couldn't live without the friendly guy with the brand-new, unwashed jeans and skill for hot-wiring cars.

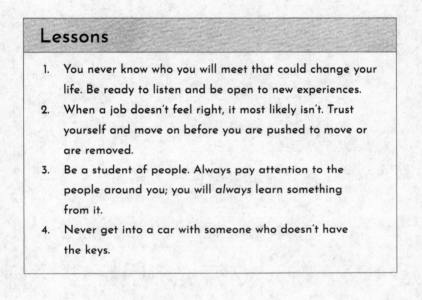

Lessons

1. You never know who you will meet that could change your life. Be ready to listen and be open to new experiences.
2. When a job doesn't feel right, it most likely isn't. Trust yourself and move on before you are pushed to move or are removed.
3. Be a student of people. Always pay attention to the people around you; you will *always* learn something from it.
4. Never get into a car with someone who doesn't have the keys.

three

Are We Doing This Together?

I RETURNED TO SEATTLE FROM DUTCH Harbor with the intention of finishing my degree. I took an evening class at Seattle Pacific University, the first of three courses I needed to complete my bachelor's degree, and started a job as a department manager for cosmetics and fragrance for a national chain in the Silverdale, Washington, store, about an hour west of Seattle by ferry.

A cosmetics department was an odd place for me in many ways. First, I had never worn much makeup and had little interest in keeping up with the latest fashion trends. Second, the department had a unique management structure within the company. It was the only department in the store where the store employed the manager, and the employees all worked for the specific brand they supported. Each of the manufacturers leased counter space and provided staff for their areas. My job was to manage the chaos created by all of the individual stakeholders and to unify everyone assigned to the makeup and fragrance department around store policies, promotions, and the store's master brand. I had to find the sweet spot that made the brand representatives want to listen to me and comply with store policies even though I had no leverage over their compensation or employment status. Getting people to follow you instead of telling them that you are the leader based on your title is a skill I would use and refine throughout my career.

I am a relationship-based person at the core. Moving from place to place, living in a motel, and changing schools often helped me to develop interpersonal skills. My go-to tool for success in professional and personal life is to develop a relationship as a foundation for all engagement. I start with finding common ground and build a vision of shared goals and relatable experience from there. Once the foundation is in place, it smooths the way to create more meaningful and useful interactions.

I had little in common with the manufacturers' reps in my charge. They were paid to look glamorous and followed current trends. They also were enthusiastic, articulate, and knowledgeable about the world of fashion. Their fantastic, and often big, hair reflected mid-eighties style, and they always wore flawless makeup. This department was a personal challenge for me. I had just spent three weeks in the Aleutian Islands of Alaska, living above a fish-processing plant with my scientist boyfriend.

Given our very diverse existence, there was little chance of finding that kernel of common ground to build on, so I adapted my approach. I decided that I would play up our differences and became a point of interest to my team. We were all in our early- or mid-twenties and mostly women, which could set the stage for fierce competition. My strategy was *not* to compete. Instead, I used the fact that we approached our jobs from opposite sides of the universe to my advantage. I was responsible for scheduling and setting up for the never-ending sales promotions and ensuring that the department reported daily revenue, and that each of the counters' tills balanced. I needed and depended on the brand reps to make all of these things happen. So I became their face to experiment on. Whenever any of the reps returned from a manufacturer's demonstration on a new makeup application or steps to create the latest look, I was first in line to be the test case. They painted on layers of eyeliner, put every type of false eyelash, and tried out every color of foundation, eye shadow, and lipstick imaginable on me. I wore them all proudly for whatever was left of my shift and returned the following day with my signature blank-canvas face. My ability to endure all types of practice sessions earned the team's respect.

My alternative approach cleared the way for effective teamwork and for everyone to contribute in a unique way that delivered successful business results and created some unlikely friendships. Against all the odds, we developed a mutual respect for one another and had a bit of fun at work.

The ferry commute to Silverdale, class two nights a week, and homework was a grueling schedule. I was moving forward in my life on several fronts but was exhausted and desperately missed Doug. As summer ended, I was promoted and moved to a larger store that allowed me to drive to work.

Meanwhile, Doug returned to Seattle in September with big news. He had been offered a job in the Philippines starting a new shrimp-farming operation. He was ready to get out of Alaska, and it was just the type of dream job he wanted. He would be the lead on the first project in the Philippines. Once that project was up and running, the model would be repeated in Thailand.

He was excited about the opportunity and started planning a move to the Philippines. The first few weeks he was home, we saw little of each other. I was working and attending class, and he was busy wrapping things up on the Alaska job and starting to nail down details of the shrimp farm in Asia.

It was a beautiful afternoon, and we were enjoying some of the warm fall weather at Golden Gardens Beach when Doug shared his plan for starting the new job. We would both go to the Philippines to get settled in, then return to the States to get married. This discussion was the first real moment of truth in our relationship. Our relationship had developed over time, and we had gotten to know each other through our long journal letters. We had talked about getting married while I was visiting Dutch Harbor, and I had accompanied him to Pittsburgh for Christmas the year before to meet his family. Doug had changed his permanent address to my apartment in Seattle. We had similar hopes and dreams and truly and enjoyed each other. He was a stabilizing influence in my life, yet shared my sense of adventure. He had grown up in a completely different environment and made me feel safe and loved.

I was turning twenty-three in a week, and an opportunity to live in Asia sounded fantastic. But I knew that I was not moving around the world without being married. I needed that commitment to make this big of a move. I had been outside of the country one time in my life, the trip to Canada with Doug the week we met, but this was something altogether different. I was not about to go to a completely foreign country without a legal attachment. All of these thoughts were rushing through my head until I blurted out that I wouldn't go unless we were married first. Time stood still. There was a long pause before he answered that he needed to think about it.

My head was spinning. *Think about it?* He had just sold me on this plan that would completely change our lives. I would have to drop out of school and walk away from my job, and he had to *think* about it? What did it matter if we got married before we left or after we got there? I have always been decisive, and from the moment the words came out of my mouth, I was sure that getting married and moving halfway around the world was the right thing for us to do. But as a result of his hesitation, there was tension in the air, and uncertainty swirled around us.

Two agonizing days passed. By the evening of the second day, we had resumed a strained but somewhat normal rhythm of life and were having a drink at one of our favorite dive bars. Doug casually asked if I had my checkbook with the calendar in it with me. I pulled the checkbook out of my purse, asking why he needed a calendar. His response was simple. He said, "We need to find a date to get married."

There it was, my marriage proposal, simple, straightforward, and matter-of-fact. It was the same tone he would use when discussing where we should have dinner or if we should take a bike ride. The same even and calm delivery that would set the tone of our lives. He would later laugh about making me wait the two days and said that he knew in an instant that we would be married but wanted to exercise his last bit of independence and carry on the façade that he was in control of our relationship. We looked at the calendar and settled on Friday, October 10, seventeen days from that moment, twenty days before we would leave Seattle.

The next few weeks were a blur. There was no way to finish the current school term, so I withdrew from the fall quarter. I gave notice at my job, and we filled out passport applications and applied for a marriage license. Planning a wedding in two weeks is crazy, and neither of us was big on ceremony. We called the courthouse and asked for any judge available on the afternoon of Friday, October 10. We then went to Macy's to find a dress and sport coat. Once we had a time and date secured with Seattle Municipal Court, we called our families. As expected, the first question was, "When is the baby due?" The first baby arrived five years later.

We had expected a small ceremony in the judge's chambers with a few local friends followed by celebratory drinks. We didn't count on family and friend from Hawaii to Pittsburgh showing up. So many were in attendance that we ended up filling the jury box and the first few rows of the spectator gallery in the courtroom. The Friday afternoon event was followed by a somewhat impromptu house party complete with our parents' willing participation in several rounds of limbo, and well-wishers serenading us with the Steeler fight song. It was a whirlwind wedding weekend that set the tone for what would become a theme of spontaneity throughout our lives.

All Aboard

Within a few days of the wedding, we were on the way to Hawaii to meet with the investors backing the venture Doug had signed on with and leveraging the time as a short honeymoon. Paychecks had not yet started for this new job, and our visas for the Philippines were in process. So, without having tremendous reserves, we stayed with a college buddy of Doug's and his girlfriend in Honolulu. As it turns out, it was a lucky choice. It was the fall of 1986, and within a week of our arrival in Honolulu, the once stable, American-friendly government in the Philippines descended into chaos. The country was in disarray after the president, Ferdinand Marcos, was overthrown.

This situation had an immediate impact on our plans. The investors pulled their support for the Philippines project and scrambled to start the second-phase project in Thailand. Two years of planning and investment had gone into the Philippines project, so there was interest in salvaging as much of that work as possible for implementation in Thailand. But there had been no groundwork done to explore the viability or the level of investment needed for the second project.

We had been in Honolulu for three weeks, and our welcome at Doug's college buddy and his girlfriend's tiny apartment was wearing out. We decided to take a gamble and go to Thailand. We would do the early feasibility work and get the ball rolling to set up the shrimp-farming project and entice the investors to come back in. The company was supportive of the plan and agreed to reimburse us for the travel costs. We had little responsibility, and this seemed like a fantastic opportunity, so we jumped in with both feet.

We found cheap seats on a charter flight from Honolulu to Tokyo that had been contracted by a Japanese school, so we would only pay a commercial fare on the Tokyo-to-Bangkok portion of the trip. Leaving most of our belongings in Hawaii, only taking a backpack each, off we went. Our second trip out of the country.

When we landed in Bangkok, it was nighttime. We found a bus to the city and relied on the driver's guidance in our hotel search. We trusted the bus driver and got off at one of the first stops. We walked across the street to a hotel he pointed out. Check-in was quick, and we were escorted to our room by one of the dozen or so guys hanging around the lobby.

I was thrilled with the prospect of sleeping horizontally after two long flights and went immediately into the bathroom to get ready for bed. When I came back into the room, Doug was sitting on the bed with the young man who had accompanied us to our room. Doug had a strange look on his face. We got rid of the young man as quickly as possible. Then Doug shared that as soon as I'd shut the bathroom door, the guy flipped over the book of tours he had been showing us and showed Doug a selection of girls to rent while he was in Thailand. Doug thanked him and told him that he had brought his own, to which the man suggested that he might want more than one for his trip. We were *so naïve*!

The shrimp project was targeted for an area approximately a hundred miles south of Bangkok, so we headed south on a train to the small beach town of Hua Hin. We ate at food stalls along the seawall and visited local temples called wats for the next few days to get our bearings. On the second day in town, we met a young man named Peanut. He approached us and asked if he could accompany us for the afternoon to practice his English. This opportunity was a wonderful gift, and Peanut became our guide for the next two weeks. Peanut was showing us the country from the inside. We had a front-row seat to the good, bad, and the reality of life in a developing nation long before it became a tourist destination. He explained the significance of many of the local wats and sacred monuments. He took us to his parents' home and introduced us to his mother and shared local, home-cooked cuisine. He negotiated taxi fees and went with us to look at potential future shrimp-farm sites. Doug and I shared a sense of adventure and relished the things we were learning. We realized that the experiences we had each day were beyond our wildest imagination.

On one of our afternoon trips into the countryside, we planned to visit caves and stop by a fishing village on the way home. Once

Peanut and the driver agreed to a price, we climbed into the back of a small pickup, joining the other half-dozen riders sitting on benches and carrying live chickens and groceries.

After several stops, we were the only three passengers in the truck. The driver stopped and demanded double the fare to take us to our destination. The situation was tense. It was clear that the driver had no intention of backing down, and we had absolutely no idea what to do. We didn't have double the cash to pay, so he demanded that we get out of the truck and drove away, leaving the three of us standing in the middle of the road miles from anywhere.

We tried to take our cues from Peanut; he was mad but didn't seem concerned. I wished we could have shared this sentiment. We were acutely aware of being in a very remote area in a country where we didn't understand the language and that we had no experience with this type of situation. Doug squeezed my hand to remind me that we were in this together, and we followed Peanut down the road toward our original destination.

We walked through the heat and dust most of the afternoon, the occasional military truck creeping slowly past us, solidifying our sense of dread. We came to a military checkpoint, and as Peanut explained our situation, several of the men operating the post motioned Doug aside and formed a tight circle around me. I was terrified. They touched my bare arms and plucked out strands of my hair. This was not a tourist area, and I was not a local. I was terrified and hoped that they finished with me quickly, and they would eventually let us go. It felt like an eternity standing there feeling exposed and vulnerable. But after a couple of minutes with no explanation, they backed away, motioning for us to continue down the road. My heart pounded, and I grabbed Doug's hand and had to keep myself from breaking into a full run. The experience made us acutely aware of our vulnerability. We were in a foreign land and needed to be more respectful and thoughtful about the decisions we made and the situations they could lead to.

In the end, the trip was worth it. The caves were magnificent, untouched, and unique.

THE OTHER LOCALS that we came into close contact with were the monkeys that lived at the wat on the top of a steep hill on the outskirts of Hua Hin. The first time we encountered them was walking up the more than two hundred steps to the wat entrance. We were coming from the market, and I was carrying a small plastic bag with fruit and snacks for the day. I felt a tug on the bag and turned, expecting to see Doug offering to take it. Instead, it was a troop of monkeys, surrounding us and holding tight to the bag to pull it away from me. Startled, I jumped back and surrendered the bag with little resistance.

The next time we met the monkey troop was more eventful. We were leaving Hua Hin and heading farther south to the island of Koh Samui in the South China Sea. Now it's full of high-end resorts, but in 1986 it was just a small jungle island with grass huts to rent for two dollars a day. We left our backpacks locked up at the train station in Hua Hin and headed to the gazebo on the seawall to relax and read for a few hours before boarding an all-night train down the coast.

As was our practice, we had picked up snacks for dinner and put them in the day pack. Suddenly, without any noise or warning, we were surrounded by monkeys in the gazebo. In the blink of an eye, the leader of the troop had grabbed for the day pack and was in an all-out tug-of-war with Doug.

Unlike the plastic bag, this pack was not easy to let go as it contained our money and passports. While Doug dueled with the sizable male monkey, I jumped up on the bench and began to scream and wave my arms wildly. Doug was able to get his hand into the pocket of the pack and extract a bag of peanuts. As he pulled them from the backpack, the container broke, and they scattered everywhere, sending most of our tormentors after the small brown nuts littering the floor of the gazebo.

The next item out of the pack was a lime, and he tossed it over the head of the alpha male to distract him long enough to empty all the food items from the backpack and throw them over the twenty-foot seawall. Survival instincts took over. I jumped on Doug's back from my perch on the bench, and we escaped out the gangway of the gazebo to the road.

As soon as we cleared the door, I sprinted back to the train station, only looking back once to see if my new husband was safe from the invading pack of primates. I was new to the vows of "till death do us part" and didn't have any interest in sticking around to ensure I lived up to them.

> I was new to the vows of "till death do us part" and didn't have any interest in sticking around to ensure I lived up to them.

Who Are You Going to Call?

Navigating everyday life in a foreign land can be exhilarating and taxing. Managing this while facing the challenge of a new cultural context, a new job, and a new marriage came with some tough lessons in the first several months. It is common practice to share your experiences with friends to gather input and perspective as you learn how to blend your lives as two individuals into a compatible couple.

Many of the attributes that attracted you to someone in the first place are the very things to perplex you when faced with a lifetime of living together. All couples work through this adjustment period. This building of a joint life was something many of our friends were experiencing at the same time, but they were doing it seven thousand miles away.

If we fought about something, it wasn't possible to give it a rest and have a girls' night out to commiserate. Or to call a friend for moral support. All we had was each other 24/7! The only way to get past these partnership speed bumps was to head directly through them. I had to find a way to work through my emotions, and the two of us had to come to some conclusion. This process was frustrating and terrifying, and it formed the foundation of our relationship.

Doug and I came from very different backgrounds and upbringings. Our ideas of normal relationship behavior were vastly different. He came from a very traditional family unit; his mother and father were in a stable marriage and, by all accounts, had a healthy relationship.

I had little experience with healthy relationships. I was insecure and defensive when we disagreed. My relationship role models had not been great. My impression of a wife's role in marriage was that you needed to speak up and defend yourself even if it was hurtful to your partner to avoid being weak and getting hurt. At no time should you be dominated by your husband.

I wanted a different type of relationship, so through these early small struggles, I slowly began to learn to listen, hold my tongue, and not say things that couldn't be taken back. However, this took a while and, without a way to rally my friends to shore up my feelings, Doug and I had to work out our differences together and begin to find our rhythm as equal parties making up a couple. Most people are not fortunate enough to have the experience of isolation to work out the foundation of their marriage without input or interference. It was a gift for us.

After several months of traveling around Southeast Asia, it had become clear that the shrimp-farm investors were not going to fund the Thailand stage of the project, so it was time for us to go home.

We had seen and experienced a lot in our travels and needed time to digest all of it.

As we sat in the departure area of the Bangkok airport, anxious to get on the plane, a man approached us. He explained that he was from India and that he and his colleague—pointing to a woman sitting a few rows over behind two large baskets covered with blankets—were missionaries. They were taking babies that had been adopted by American families in Seattle to their new parents. He shared the official-looking paperwork listing each child and the name and address of their new parents.

The flight was long, and they had seven babies to care for on the journey. He asked if we would be willing to help by holding a baby. He explained that he and his colleague would manage the diaper changing and had all the supplies needed; it was just a matter of keeping the baby with us. We agreed to help and told him our seat numbers.

Adopting babies from Asia had grown in popularity since the end of the Vietnam War eleven years earlier. All of the paperwork would be completed by low-quality international phone calls and faxing official papers back and forth. When the US visa for the child being adopted was approved, it included a transit visa for a representative from the adoption agency to travel with the child to the United States. At the time, Americans didn't travel internationally as frequently or as casually as they do today, and Southeast Asia was not a tourist destination. It was much easier for the agency to obtain this short-term visa for one of their employees who spoke English to accompany a child than it was for the adoptive parents to navigate a foreign country to pick up their child.

Once the plane took off, the man appeared in the aisle and handed a tiny little human named Megan to us. Holding this child brought all of the emotions of our last several months to the surface. We had seen extraordinary sites, been welcomed into homes that were little more than grass-covered lean-tos, tasted food that I would have never imagined, and seen poverty and suffering that can't be explained. This baby was at the intersection of all of those experiences. Having her in my arms even if only for the flight was like bringing a piece of all we had learned and experienced home with me. It was a way to connect our new awareness of the world to the familiar homeland we were returning to.

When we landed in Seattle, we had the honor of presenting Megan to her family. It was a rapid exchange, but it left an impression on us that would later guide the choices we made in building our own family. It was a beautiful end to our adventure.

Lessons

1. Leadership is about having people want to follow you, rather than focusing on how you will lead them.
2. The foundation of leadership is to create a relationship by identifying common ground to build on.
3. Speak up for what you want, even if it means risking something or someone you care about. Living with uncertainty is just as bad as living with thoughts of "what if." Risk can be healthy and result in a better outcome than simply settling.
4. Being a couple doesn't mean giving up yourself. Instead, learn how to use your best qualities to complement another person.

5. Be open to the people around you. People will provide the most unexpected experiences, many of which will have influences on your life that you may not realize until much later on.

four

The Working World

OUR FIRST TASTE OF LIFE outside the United States was a heady one. It had all of the makings for years of great stories: high adventure, including a tug-of-war with a monkey over a day pack, being dropped off in the middle of nowhere by a taxi, spending time with locals and their families, and having the honor of delivering a baby to her new country and family. The time we spent in Southeast Asia was a prelude to the rest of our lives. The travel exposed me to endless learning opportunities, languages, cultures, food, and how to navigate life in entirely unfamiliar environments. It was a fantastic time, but the reality of our financial situation could not be ignored. Doug's hopes of leading the development of aquaculture in Southeast Asia had not worked out. We were broke, tired, and needed a way to earn a living. We needed to grow up and start being adults in the working world.

We landed in Seattle on a cold, gray early spring day and headed for our apartment that we had subleased to my best friend, Carrie. It was a small studio, so we only stayed a few days before beginning a tour of couch surfing and house sitting. Because it was so small, moving back into the apartment for the long term was not an option. We had agreed that Carrie could live there for at least eighteen months, so she had relocated from Colorado and taken over the lease and all expenses.

I reconnected with George, my first landlord in Seattle. He always needed extra hands for his housecleaning business, and it was a quick income. Doug reconnected with his contacts in the Alaskan fishing community, and within a few weeks, he was on his way back to Dutch Harbor for a three-month contract. Working in the Bering Sea was a dangerous way to make a living, but it offered income that we needed to rent an apartment and start our lives again in Seattle. We were both clear that the jobs we were doing were short-term. These jobs were a way for us to earn a living but represented a step back for both of us. I never imagined I would be a maid at this stage of my life.

I'm Not a Salesperson!

I worked on George's housecleaning crew three or four days a week and applied for permanent jobs on my days off. The internet did not exist, so the application process was labor-intensive, including typing and copying my résumé, and dropping it off in person to prospective employers. I registered with employment and temp agencies and took the required typing tests.

There were two sizable commercial photo labs in Seattle, and I dropped off applications to both. One of the labs was in the middle of an expansion. They had moved into new facilities, hired a new COO, and were looking to expand their business. They hired me as an outside salesperson. This was the first job I had with a cubicle, business cards, and a sales quota.

To say I was lost would be a vast understatement. There were four people on the outside sales team: Randy, Ginger, Bud, and me. Randy was a little older, and much more of a born salesman than me. Randy had come with the new COO, George, from his last company, and they were both wheeler-dealers. They talked fast, could make anything sound viable, and made you believe you couldn't live another day without purchasing whatever they were selling. George was tall and skinny and wore big glasses, circa 1975. His enormous ears stuck straight out from his head like handlebars, and he always had a cigarette in his hand. He was loud with a very distinctive laugh that could be heard all over the building. Everyone knew when George had left the building. Things got quiet.

Randy, on the other hand, was short and round. They were like the odd couple. Randy always smiled, made friends fast, and could charm anyone into a sales order. He was a guy that you trusted and wanted to do business with.

Ginger was about ten years older than me and had worked her way up at the lab. Over the years, she had done almost every job in the company and knew everyone in the local industry. She was sweet, friendly, and a complete scatterbrain. Ginger was assigned the task of training me and showing me the ropes. Training meant spending the first few weeks riding around in her car, meeting customers. She never seemed to sell them anything or engage in anything resembling a sales conversation; instead, she was a problem-solver and used her in-depth knowledge of the lab's capabilities to ensure that her customers got the product they needed. She used the same skills to motivate the lab teams to deliver on commitments she made to customers. Her work was always on time and available for delivery. Ginger's communication style still mystifies me, but her relationship formula was genius. She was the original solution salesperson.

Then there was Bud. Bud was "old school." He was in his late forties—ancient to me at the time—and very traditional. For years, he was the only outside salesperson for the lab. He was set in his ways and moved at his own pace. He cultivated his customers with long lunches, golf games, and monthly poker nights with the guys. He wore polyester suits, carried a briefcase, and didn't see any reason to change the sales process he had used for the past fifteen years. Ginger had been Bud's assistant before taking on clients of her own, and he preferred to have her work based on his direction. There had been no need to have a formal customer segmentation with just the two salespeople. When there was a big order, Bud managed it, and Ginger supported it. That's the way it had always been.

Randy and I doubled the size of the sales team and changed the landscape just by walking into the building. The industry was changing quickly, and to the owner's credit, he knew that the lab needed to innovate to stay relevant. Photo enlargements and photographic products had not yet gone digital, but it was coming quickly, and new revenue streams were required to keep the lights on.

George's approach was anything but by the book. He swore loudly, told dirty and offensive jokes, and had no regard for anyone's personal feelings. He was also the most caring and impactful teacher/manager I had in my early career. He had worked for several mid-sized companies in Washington State as a sales and business development leader and knew people from all walks of life. With this experience, he confidently set a new direction for the lab, targeting commercial businesses and prioritizing new opportunities over support for local photographers and artists. Building an outside sales team, with monthly quotas and segmented accounts, was step one. Step two was training the sales team to upsell and cross-sell.

It was against this background that I learned some of the most valuable lessons of my life. George pushed me headfirst into the first tentative steps of self-advocacy and negotiation. I had accepted the sales job based on a compensation package with an 80 percent base salary and a 20 percent commission. I thought this was a good deal that enabled me to plan living expenses on the base number with the additional 20 percent as a windfall. I had never worked on commission and was terrified to try.

As George went to work building a commercial sales team, the first thing to go was an 80 percent base salary. He believed that commission motivated salespeople to work harder and sell more, so with only a few months on the job, he announced in our morning sales meeting that our compensation packages were changing. We would still have an 80/20 split, but the 80 percent would be a commission, based on a set sales quota, and the 20 percent would be a base salary. The news of this change put me into a tailspin. How could I ever sell enough to eat? I had no experience in selling and next to no confidence that I could pull this off. I was a mess.

It took a few days, but I got up the courage to go to George's office and tell him I needed to talk about the compensation change. I closed the door, sat down, and immediately dissolved into tears. How in the world was I going to pay rent, groceries, and gas with only 20 percent of my salary?

He took a deep breath, lit a cigarette, leaned back in his chair, and stretched his long legs out with his feet on the desk, trying to hide a smile. He calmly asked me what in the world I was talking about earning only 20 percent of my salary? Then he explained that, in fact, he saw the change in the exact opposite way and that I would be making way more money with this commission scheme.

He told me about his experience as a young man starting in sales. His first goal was to make an annual income number equal to his age (in thousands). He quickly achieved that and moved his personal goal to double his age, and so on. As we talked, I warmed to this idea. I loved it. For me, that would mean an annual income of $24,000. That seemed like a doable number and one that wasn't nearly as scary as 80 percent commission sounded. I started to do mental multiplication and dream about how many times I could multiply my age into an annual salary. In this context, there was no salary cap.

During our discussion, I calmed down and began to get more interested and excited about the vision of potential wealth that George had laid out for me, but I was still worried. This was a significant change, and I had few tools and little experience to work with to make this a reality. As he lit another cigarette, knowing that I was still on edge, George offered a compromise: my compensation would not be switched to 80 percent commission overnight. Instead, each month for the next six months, the percentage of base salary would decrease, and the portion of the commission would increase. I could live with this; it would give me time to adjust and to learn sales skills.

The discussions with George over my compensation taught me a few essential lessons, starting with the fact that you don't have to take the first offer without discussion or negotiation. The change to the salary plan was not presented as a choice to the team but, without realizing it, I had started a negotiation. By mustering the courage to raise the issue, I was able to express my concern and open the door and pave the way for an adjustment that I could live with. And my having the guts to raise a complicated subject gave George faith in my ability to manage in a tough sales situation. I had self-advocated for the first time, and although it was certainly not smooth, it was a big step forward in my professional and personal development. Thank goodness I had a helpful and experienced manager that could just as quickly have shown me the door but chose to invest in me instead.

A FEW WEEKS after my compensation discussion with George, we arrived in the meeting room to find a video camera set up on a tripod next to the conference table. We were going to role-play a sales call, videotape it, and watch and critique each other's skills and abilities. My first thought was, "*Are you kidding me!*" I started feeling sick to my stomach. I had dropped a class in college on the day I found out that I would be required to stand up in front of the class and give a speech. The course was full of people I didn't know and carried little risk, but I was still so terrified that I dropped the class.

The idea of performing in front of a camera was much worse! This was an up close and personal opportunity to look like a fool in front of my coworkers. These people were my in-house competitors; there was no way in the world I was going to subject myself to that kind of ridicule. I did the only mature, logical thing: I burst into tears and ran out of the building. I sat outside for a lifetime, or roughly forty-five minutes. I needed to come up with a new plan for my life and a way to earn a living. I couldn't stand in front of a group, much less a camera, and speak. Sales calls were different. Talking with a customer meant engaging in a real conversation, so I was confident that I had the skills to perform when it counted. This exercise was designed to make people look stupid. I sat outside long enough that I assumed the hellish role-play experiment was over, and I could get on with my real sales calls.

| This exercise was designed to make people look stupid.

I was not that lucky. The meeting was still going, and the team was waiting for me to come back in and take my turn at the role-play. Everyone else on the team had done it and endured group feedback on what they did well and what needed improvement, and had shared ideas and approaches to increase sales. I had no option but to sit down and get on with it. It was terrible. I was so nervous I couldn't think straight. It was clear immediately that I didn't have the first clue how to handle objections or how to listen to what the customer was telling me, or the skills to solve their problems with creative solutions. All I knew how to do was introduce myself and share a list of services.

I got through the exercise, and I don't remember any of the specific feedback, but I know it wasn't easy to hear. This role-play was the first of many experiences that taught me to slow down my initial reaction and think a few steps beyond my first impulse to panic and flee. I was going to have to accept that I would have to do things that pushed me out of my comfort zone to gain much-needed professional skills. Looking back, I see just how little self-confidence I had. I have always been able to appear confident and fearless, but the reality is I was (and am) often terrified.

* * *

OTHER THAN THE role-play experiment, most aspects of my sales career were looking up. I did have a few missteps that still make me laugh, even though they are among the most embarrassing moments of my life. One of the perks of being an outside commercial salesperson was an expense account. A large part of my job was developing relationships with purchasing department leaders, production managers, and decision-makers. The first-line tool for this was the business lunch.

I took people to lunch almost every day, and it was during one of these lunch meetings that I had the most horrific fashion accident in my life. George and I had invited a vice president of one of our largest customers to lunch at a very expensive restaurant. The restaurant was known for long, boozy lunches where deals were made, so we were thrilled that they had accepted our invitation.

It was summer, and I had dressed for the occasion in a two-piece dress. The base piece was a spaghetti strap dress made of slip material three-quarters of the way down, which transitioned to a white linen pleated skirt with a big red stripe going all the way around the center. The top that was to go over the slip portion was a red, short-sleeved, very tailored jacket that came to the top of the skirt. I topped it off with navy and white spectator shoes. I looked great.

I was driving, and George hopped in the back seat to let the customer sit in the front. As I sat down in the driver's seat after picking up our customer, I felt one of the straps on my dress snap, and the slippery material started to slide down my body as I drove. I was startled but quickly realized that we could valet park at the restaurant, and I would hold my handbag close to my body and make it to the table. No one would be the wiser.

It had worked perfectly, and lunch was going well, but just as the conversation headed in the right direction, I shifted in my seat and felt the other strap pop; and the dress slid down to my waist. All I could think of was how in the world I could get out of the restaurant with my dress around my ankles. When it was time to leave, I slowly stood up from the table and held on to my dress, walking to the car. George paid the valet attendant, and as soon as I dropped the customer off at his office, he turned to me, irritated, and asked, "What the hell was wrong with you at lunch?" I explained my dress dilemma and thought that we would both die laughing. We got the deal, and I have carried safety pins in my handbag ever since that day.

> All I could think of was how in the world I could get out of the restaurant with my dress around my ankles.

All Hands on Deck

In the course of my sales rounds, I developed relationships with marketing managers all over the city. One of those was with Pam, a marketing manager for a regional drugstore chain. Pam had a bigger-than-life personality. She was tall, beautiful, smart, outspoken, and fun. The company that Pam worked for held the second position in the local market and was outdone regularly by the hometown family-owned market leader.

She had a big job to do and was always open to new ideas to brighten up the retail stores and create a unique look that would attract young customers to high-margin departments in the stores.

We had several things in common and often combined our mutual ambition, creativity, and willingness to take risks to get things done. It was this friendship and mutual respect that hatched a plan that would be the lab's biggest and most ambitious order ever—and would give me the experience and confidence I needed to move my career forward.

Pam was struggling with how to increase the appeal and sales for the beauty department of the stores. Beauty products and makeup were high-margin areas, and she needed to create a shopping experience that would feel more upscale, but not as expensive as a department store. Most importantly, she had to bring more women into the beauty department.

I had the idea to install huge photos of the cosmetic manufacture models all over the beauty section of the stores. We could create a store-within-a-store using images that were already available from the vendors. Drugstores are full of manufacturer materials: cheap signs with weekly sales and coupon offers. Creating a more permanent, high-end look and feel to the beauty and makeup department would make a statement, and the department would stand out from the rest of the store. Pam liked the idea and agreed to a prototype store to test out the concept.

George loved the idea and agreed to do the sample store for free. We selected a high-traffic store in the heart of the city and produced huge three-by-five-foot enlargements of four images. We mounted them to foam core boards and constructed a snap-on frame. We then attached the photo with Velcro or double-sided tape so that we could swap out the images. This reusable base allowed the drugstore to stay current with trends and provided a recurring revenue stream for the lab. It worked brilliantly! Traffic and sales went up in the sample store and gave us the data we needed to show the drugstore executives that this approach appealed to their target audience and set them apart from the competition.

The company had 119 stores in Washington and a few in Idaho. The stores came in three size configurations, which meant that the order I sold included over seven hundred of the largest format products that the lab offered, plus the frame system. The result would be the new revenue stream that the lab needed.

We sold this concept up the leadership ladder at the drugstore, and several of their suppliers signed on to fund the project. It was a win on all sides. The test was one thing, but going into a production process of this scale was a completely different ballgame. As they say, the devil is in the details, and that proved accurate for this project.

Assembly of the complex photo stands required time, and installation could only happen after hours. It was an all-hands-on-deck event, and Pam and I recruited all our friends to help.

We turned an unfinished portion of the lab into an assembling and staging area and hosted late-night pizza parties for anyone that would help. We created assembly teams that would complete two or three stores per night. Weekend install trips to eastern Washington and Idaho resulted in all-night work parties followed by sleeping all day. It was a ton of work, but in the end, we repositioned the makeup department and drove a significant increase in department traffic and sales. Success! I no longer needed to worry about my commission split. George had been right all along. I needed to relax, listen, and learn. I hit the first salary goal we had talked about, and I started to find my feet professionally.

Lessons

1. Being pushed out of your comfort zone is where learning happens. Doing new things is hard for everyone. Don't opt out of trying.

2. Don't take an offer at face value. Ninety-nine percent of the time, there is room for negotiating. In the business world, accepting the first offer is most often seen as the easy way out. If you believe in your position, test the waters with a counterproposal. The worst that can happen is you are turned down.

3. Negotiation doesn't have to be adversarial. By raising questions, you start a discussion, and before you know it, you are negotiating.

4. Self-advocating is a life skill that everyone should practice. It is easier said than done in many cases, but you will always feel better if you have represented yourself honestly. Note that presentation is everything here, and tone matters.

5. Innovation is often welcome and a game changer. Thinking out of the box can be a huge win. Start by recruiting allies that can help you sell the idea. Set realistic targets and test before going big.

five

Madison Avenue Seattle Style

When I Say It, You Do It

The drugstore cosmetics department project had paid off. It gave me the confidence that I could be a great salesperson and provided proof that I was innovative and could develop effective professional relationships. The visibility of the project also gave me a positive reputation in the local marketing community. Pam was receiving accolades for thinking outside the box and disrupting retail merchandising practice. I was receiving calls from other retailers and prospective customers asking for me to come and work with them to develop visual solutions. To my delight, one of those calls was from a local advertising firm.

The call was from Brems Eastman, a small, locally owned marketing and ad agency. The production manager was an older man named Stan, who had been in the ad business all of his life. He had a dry sense of humor and knew, or had seen, everything in the ad business. Stan was known around town for his quick wit and no-nonsense approach. We hit it off immediately. Within a few months of working together on photo projects, he mentioned that the agency was looking to replace an account executive, and I jumped at the opportunity. Working for an ad agency sounded much more fun and glamorous than working as a commercial salesperson for a photo lab.

Brems Eastman was a partnership between Chris Brems, the creative director and all-around fatherly figure, and Sue Eastman, a young, talented, temperamental writer. They had been in business for several years. When I started, they had twenty employees, a few anchor clients under retainer, and were always looking for new business.

Stan, the production manager, made introductions to both Chris and Sue. I interviewed, and within a few weeks I moved into my first private office with my name on the door and business cards with the title *Account Executive*. I was over the moon. It was hard to leave the lab, George, and the sales team I had grown to appreciate and enjoy, but to move to an agency would mean that I was now a customer of the lab. How much better could this get?

Like most agencies, Brems Eastman was a house divided. Chris was the quiet, calm part of the duo. He kept the balance in the agency, always smiled, and was coach and mentor to all. He only met with select clients or showed up for pitches that required both partners to be present. Chris reviewed all the creative concepts before clients were pitched and generally provided stability to the business.

Sue was his counterbalance. She was intense, rarely smiled, and marched down the halls as if going to battle, even if it was just to the kitchen for a cup of coffee. Most of us steered clear of her, no matter what. She was smart and talented and knew how to develop a winning communications strategy or write compelling copy for any project. She had a low tolerance for mistakes and no patience for discussion—including briefing creative teams on client requirements, or reviewing work that she didn't write. Looking back, I realize we had some things in common. She was young, in over her head, and just as scared as I was. Sue had earned a reputation for being difficult and unfriendly, complete with a nickname in town among other agency teams. They called her "waterworks" because, much of the time, she was either teary-eyed or had a red, blotchy face from crying. She was just as broody and unfriendly as Chris was pleasant and warm. Somehow, together they had a thriving agency.

On my second day, I was accompanying Sue to a meeting with the agency's biggest client, a hospital located about thirty minutes south of Seattle. I learned this, along with the summary of who would be in attendance, on the drive south in Sue's red MG convertible. It was fall and chilly in Seattle, so it was loud and cold hurtling down the highway, weaving around cars twice our size. Terrifying.

Jane was the client decision-maker, with the title vice president of marketing. She had a distinct vision for branding and communication, which was not particularly innovative or interesting. Her second-in-command was an amiable, outgoing man named Lind. It was immediately apparent that Lind and I were there for support and did not have speaking roles unless responding to direct questions.

At the end of two-plus hours, we were back in the tiny red rocket on the way back to Seattle. Sue's instructions were to create a conference report from the notes I had taken by ten the next morning.

Once she had reviewed and approved the report, I was to send it on to the client as a record of our meeting. Conference reports were a staple of agency life. They contained a summary of the discussion, specifics about decisions made, and concise action items with owner names and due dates included.

These conference reports were distributed the day after each client meeting; often, they required a signature from the account team that prepared the report and the client team leader to ensure everyone was on the same page as work began. Agency business is often non-tangible, since charges to the client are based on the time people spend thinking about work. So the conference report is currency between the agency and the client. I had seen several of these in the files left for me, so I replicated the style and distributed my first conference report on time. It felt like the first win of my new job.

Thursday afternoon rolled around, and Sue showed up in my office about an hour before we were to leave for the weekly meeting with our hospital client. She was holding a copy of the conference report that I had completed the Friday before (my first one) and began running her finger down the list of action items asking me for updates on the materials that were due to the client at our meeting. I was utterly lost. I also had a copy of the conference report as a reference, and as I looked down the list she was reading, each item that was due had the name *Sue* next to it as the owner. She stood in the door to my office, turned her customary red face toward me, and shouted: "When I say I am going to do something in a client meeting, that means *you* do it."

The statement hit me like a punch in the stomach. I was already nervous about the weekly meeting and the stressful drive in the tiny red car with a sullen, grumpy boss, but this encounter wrecked me. I had no idea that I missed the critical translation that I was responsible for everything for which she took ownership during the client meeting. This would have been a great piece of information to have received a week earlier.

The car ride down was agonizing, and things got even worse as Sue explained to the client that I was new to the agency and not up to my job. This painful event was one of the most critical and impactful lessons of my career. It was my first encounter with a business hierarchy. Until this point in my young career, I had been naïve and believed that the conversation on the surface represented intention and fact.

My experience with managers had been one-to-one and transaction-oriented. My jobs came with clear goals and deliverables that were tangible and in my control. This job was more complex; the work I was doing was part of a larger team and included intellectual assets that needed to fit within a broader context. My scope had changed, and I needed to learn to work through others, both people above me and beside me in the organization.

Mastering this new paradigm required a steep learning curve and for me to be on my game at all times. I learned to listen between the lines and felt like I was learning a foreign language. When Sue agreed to a timeline, a specific deliverable, or an action, I was to ensure it happened. While the style of this lesson was not constructive, the net result was a skill I would use almost every day in every single job I had from that point on.

Learning to understand and interpret the nuance of professional meeting conversation is a competency that's critical to success, but almost impossible to learn without taking some serious hard knocks in the process. Being able to fully comprehend when to take action yourself and when to work through others is core to success, no matter what size of team or organization. Accountability and credit are tricky to navigate but a skill worth the time and attention to master.

Sue and Chris were well entrenched as good-cop bad-cop, and each had their following and loyalists within the agency. Learning this unwritten organizational structure was helpful, and it could be leveraged by account teams to get the work needed.

About a year into my job, Chris and Sue called everyone into the conference room to announce we were going to merge with another agency. Brems Eastman would become Brems Eastman Glade, and with this merger would come new clients and new people in every department. The merger was unexpected and pushed our small but somewhat dysfunctional team directly into unknown territory. We knew and understood how to manage Chris and Sue, but adding a third player into management would change the game entirely.

Ultimately, the choice to merge had a positive impact on the overall business. Glade brought clients and talent that enabled us to expand and attract new business. The team from Glade had in-depth skills in broadcast and media planning that complemented the more innovative creative talent we had in place.

After a few years at the agency, my personal life started showing signs of maturing. Doug had stopped working in Alaska and started a position working for a Japanese trading company in their Seattle office. His job was to source and buy seafood across North America and ship it to Japan. This was the ideal position for Doug at the time as it allowed him to travel and to keep his hand in the seafood industry without having to work in dangerous conditions. His new employers were anxious to get to know all about Doug, including meeting me. I was invited to join him on his first business trip to Tokyo.

Doug was slated to meet the executives at the company, then spend five days touring seafood markets and processing plants across Japan. I was to meet the executives, then pack my dress and pumps into my backpack and begin the trip I had mapped out following a shoestring guide travel book. We planned to meet in Kyoto at the end of the five days. We spent a few beautiful days together exploring the ancient city and dining in sushi restaurants where the fish was so fresh that I screamed when it moved on the plate. This trip was a completely different experience from the one we had had in Southeast Asia, but we loved them both.

We purchased a small house with the help of a loan from Doug's brother for the down payment and spent every spare moment and penny fixing it up. We settled into a rhythm of life that included Friday night happy hours with a group of young couples we had met over the past few years, including my old boss Barb from Generra and her husband, and Pam from the drugstore and her husband. We went skiing on winter weekends, camped together in the summer, and enjoyed regular backyard BBQs at one another's houses.

Did You Walk Here from Seattle?

I was sitting at my desk at the agency one afternoon a few weeks before Thanksgiving, and the receptionist put through a call from my predecessor, Karyn. I had never met Karyn in person but felt like I knew her well since I had inherited her clients and all of her handwritten notes and files. It was an oddly familiar yet distant relationship we shared.

I took the call immediately. She introduced herself and got right to the reason for the call. She had left the agency to work for a tech company, and now that company was looking for additional people with the same skill set for their Corporate Communications Department. She told me that even though she didn't know me, the fact that I had successfully taken on her clients and worked with Sue

Eastman for almost two years qualified me. She asked if I could come and interview the following week.

Karyn spoke highly of her employer and said that the people were young, friendly, and smart. The work was hard, with long hours, but the paycheck was more secure than at the agency, and the atmosphere was more stable and not subjective to the moods that we were both familiar with at the agency. I had nothing to lose and agreed to come in and talk with human resources. The interview was set for 11:00 a.m. the following Tuesday at the company's main office in Redmond, Washington.

Several months earlier, I had had a significant skiing accident that still required regular doctor appointments and physical therapy twice a week. I had used crutches for almost six months and was now walking unaided but wore tennis shoes with orthotics to help my recovery.

Midday would be tricky to leave the office, but a "doctor's appointment" would not seem out of the ordinary, and sixty to ninety minutes was plenty of time for an interview.

I received a package of information from the company at my home address and completed the application form that I was to bring with me on Tuesday. I filled in all of the necessary information about my employment history and references, but was stuck on the question of salary. Doug and I talked it over and figured I would go ahead and aim high. I put $27,000 in the "desired salary" box. At the time, I was earning $17,000 a year, which was an average wage for a woman working full-time. The ask of $10,000 more seemed enormous, and if I got half of it, I would have been thrilled.

On Tuesday, I dressed in a smart business-appropriate outfit with my tennis shoes. I was concerned about what they would think about my shoes for an interview but had no choice. I mentioned my

fake doctor appointment to a few people as a cover on Monday afternoon, and at ten thirty on Tuesday morning, I headed out of the
Brems Eastman office and across the lake to the Microsoft campus.

The receptionist took my coat, and I was soon sitting across the
desk from the HR person I had spoken with on the phone. After
about an hour, she asked me to follow her down the hall. We entered
a different office identical to hers, where she introduced me to a
manager from the Corporate Communications Department and left
me to talk with him. This process repeated every hour until, finally,
I was taken into a large corner office and told that the director of
corporate communications would be with me in a few minutes.

By this time, I was panicking inside. I had left my office for a
doctor's appointment, which generally lasted for about an hour.
How in the world was I going to explain my extended disappear-
ance? It was not like I could excuse myself and explain that I had
lied to my current employer to interview. It was now 5:00 p.m.,
and I had been interviewing for six hours. I had not prepared for
this process.

The director of corporate communications, Val, bounded into
her office, shook my hand, looked down at my tennis shoes, and
promptly asked if I had walked from Seattle. I answered no and
quickly mentioned a skiing accident but was anxious to move off
the topic. She responded, in a very matter-of-fact tone, that she
was not interested in hiring me for my feet. She wanted to know
how my mind worked. She wasn't the first person that had inquired
about why I was wearing tennis shoes that day, but her response
put me at ease immediately.

I got to the office early the next morning to catch up on work that
I had not finished the day before, hoping I could get away with as
few questions as possible. Just after the receptionist arrived, I

received a call from Microsoft's HR, offering me a job with a base salary of $30,000. I thought I was going to faint. She asked for a fax number to send over paperwork and said that they wanted me to start right after Thanksgiving, two weeks away. I immediately ran to the fax machine and stood there until the fax on Microsoft letterhead arrived. With a written offer in hand, I had to deal with the more practical matter of giving notice to Brems Eastman. Having seen a few others come and go in the two years I had worked there, I knew how this would play out. So, I chose to give the news to Chris and got the silent treatment from Sue from the moment she found out I was leaving until I walked out the door.

The time at Brems Eastman had been valuable on many levels. Understanding the agency business and how to manage client expectations and creative teams would be invaluable throughout my career. But the most impactful lesson I learned at the agency was what type of leader I didn't want to be. Through my time at Brems, I learned what it means to set the tone from the top.

Sue was smart and a fantastic strategist and writer, but her brooding, moody behavior gave the office an unsteady feel. You never knew how the day was going to go until you saw Sue and could gauge her mood. If she had a bad day, you needed to steer clear and keep your head down. If she was happy, she might take the whole office for lunch. This type of manic behavior took a toll.

The effect on the morale, culture, and the overall business of this lack of awareness and empathy toward employees was my biggest takeaway. Everyone loved Chris, but he never spoke up about this issue and never truly led the company and staff. To be celebrated for a specific craft or discipline is not enough to be successful or be an effective leader.

Lessons

1. Be aware of the hierarchy and power structure in an organization. When you are new, asking clarifying questions can speed your ramp time and ease the transition into the team.

2. When to take direct action and when to work through others is a critical skill to master, no matter what level you are in an organization.

3. When you see behavior that you admire, study and copy it. When you see behavior you don't respect, study it just as hard and remember not to replicate it.

4. Watching and learning from leaders, good and bad, will help you become a more effective leader.

six

"We Want You for Your Mind, Not Your Feet"

I STARTED WORK AT MICROSOFT ON Monday, December 4, 1989. At the time, the company was a medium-sized technology startup based in the suburbs of Seattle. Microsoft business was based on a partnership with IBM to develop and sell a computer operating system and coding languages that were used by developers. There were no direct sales to consumers, and unless you were a programmer or worked directly with back-end computer systems in large companies, you had never heard of Microsoft. Personal computers were not standard office tools.

The goal of the interview process was to find out how I thought and to see if I had what it took to work at Microsoft, and to be a significant contributor that possessed core values, including "intellectual horsepower." I have always been good at thinking on my feet and have more energy than most people. My bent toward independence and problem-solving seemed the right fit for both of us. I was an inexperienced interviewee, so I answered questions honestly, and while I was nervous, I felt comfortable being me. At the time, the hiring scale was heavily weighted on having energy, drive, and attitude—as opposed to later years when your academic pedigree was the key determinant for a hire/no hire decision. When I was hired at Microsoft, I was not a college graduate, and it didn't seem to matter: the company founder wasn't either. The Microsoft of today is characterized as being staffed with elite programmers educated at top universities around the world. In the early 1990s, the culture was built on high-energy people, willing to work hard with a hunger to change the world. I can't remember having conversations with colleagues about where they went to school. It didn't matter.

From the moment you walked in the door, there was a feeling of urgency and that everyone was needed. Technological and marketing talent were both required to deliver Bill Gates' vision of "a computer on every desk and in every home." There was no playbook to follow. It was up to us to write as we went. It was empowering and exciting.

There were nine people in my orientation session that Monday morning—seven men, two women. I don't remember much about the content presented other than we watched a narrated video about Bill dropping out of school and Paul, Steve, and Bill having to stop at a shopping mall early in the morning to buy a tie for Bill on the way to the first big meeting with IBM. A member of the leadership team welcomed us to the community of four thousand global employees. I was impressed.

My orientation group ate lunch as a group in the cafeteria for the first time. It looked like a casual dining restaurant. Stations were offering different foods, including a grill station, a salad bar, and the entrée of the day. It was amazing. There were large drink coolers everywhere, and the drinks were free. I had never heard of anything like this at a company lunchroom. After the meal, we wished one another well in our new adventure and headed off to our respective buildings to check in with our new managers.

I was a corporate communications specialist; my first manager was a woman named Nancy who I hadn't met during the lengthy interview process. Nancy was unique in many ways in the Microsoft context. She was about ten years older than most of the people that worked at Microsoft. (The average employee at the time was in their mid-twenties.) She dressed professionally, always in a dress or suit and high heels. She walked everywhere fast, was serious, and got to the point in every discussion. Nancy was no nonsense and had an air of getting shit done. She scared me a bit, but I admired her and used every engagement to watch and learn.

My office was in one of the newest buildings on campus. The buildings were all X shaped. The larger, more modern buildings were two Xs put together connected by a central lobby. The X shape ensured that I spent at least ten minutes lost each time I left my office, and finding the bathroom was like a treasure hunt.

Everyone at the company had an individual office with the same furnishings: a desk, floor lamp, bookcase, and guest chair. An office window signified managers or longevity at the company. Inside offices were for new or junior people. I learned not to get comfortable in an office or with a manager. Both changed often as the company worked to find its footing defining the software industry and absorbing an increasing number of new hires every week.

I joined a group of nine female CorpCom Specialists. I was given Hardware as client businesses. Hardware was a newly formed business unit with only one product that was commercially available, the Microsoft Mouse, which was sold only as a bundled product with Microsoft Paintbrush. The Apple Macintosh used a mouse to move around the screen and select items on the desktop; however, a PC mouse was used as little more than a toy or with a few niche products.

The company was gearing up for its most significant product launch to date—a new operating system that would require a mouse. The launch of this new operating system would change the industry, and the mouse was an essential element of how the software worked.

The MS Mouse had been redesigned from the ground up for this occasion. The new Microsoft Mouse would be sold with MS Paintbrush as before but would also be bundled with this new operating system and as a stand-alone product for the first time. The mouse was a big part of the operating system launch and therefore was funded for an advertising campaign that would run in industry publications alongside the new operating system campaign. The agency had been working on concepts for weeks and was ready to present.

As they did with all big launches, Microsoft brought in an ad agency to handle the launch. The agency team was in the office to present concepts for the mouse. I spent the morning as an observer with the agency and the CorpCom leadership team to agree on recommendations. Next, with our recommendations in hand, we presented them to the business unit. An ad was selected, and the media plan approved to start the same day as the scheduled operating system product launch date: April 13, 1990.

* * *

THE EXCITEMENT WAS building around the company about this revolutionary operating system, and I was thrilled to be a part of it. I was adjusting to the unique communication style, taking computer classes offered to all employees, finding interesting people to have lunch with at different themed cafeterias, and slowly beginning to find my way back to my office following each meeting.

I was the front line between the agency and our internal CorpCom creative teams. A few weeks after the agency meeting to approve the mouse advertisement, I received a package from the agency with final approved artwork for the ad to pass on to the business unit. As soon as I opened the packaging, it was clear that the illustrations inside were not the same ones that had been approved. I figured it was an error and called my counterpart at the agency to let him know and asked when the correct materials would be sent. The agency account manager was surprised to get my call and said that this was the ad that had been approved but agreed to check and call me back. The next call I received was from the account supervisor, who led the agency team. He said that he was calling to explain to me how an agency works, then told me that while the business unit had indeed liked a different advertisement, the agency team were the experts and they felt that the advertisement they had selected after the meeting would meet the needs of the product much better. He then instructed me to let the client know that a change had been made in their best interest.

I listened and took careful notes during our discussion. I had left an agency world less than thirty days before and knew the process between creatives and clients very well. I also knew from sitting in the initial meetings that the agency team preferred the ad that they were now calling "approved." This was the first big test. My actions here would establish how my internal team, my client businesses, and our vendor treated me and set the tone for my career at Microsoft. When the account supervisor finished the 101 lessons on the agency process, I thanked him and let him know that I had been hired from an agency and understood the process thoroughly. This was the first person I had run into that was truly condescending and unpleasant, and it shook me a bit, but he was from the agency, not a Microsoft coworker.

The next order of business was to locate my manager, Nancy, and let her know about the conversation and hope that I had done the right thing by pushing back. I knew that the agency account supervisor would also be in touch with Nancy and CorpCom leadership to fill them in on our conversation. Within a few hours, the department director, Val, was standing at the door to my office, asking to see the materials that the agency had sent. She took one quick look, handed them back, and said that I should expect to see the approved materials the next day from the agency. I was ecstatic. I had made the right choice to push back, but more importantly, I had joined a company and a department that would support its people. As I suspected, this had set the tone. Internally with Microsoft teams, I had earned respect and proved that I was a trusted partner. Unfortunately, the agency team did not feel the same: they were cautious and a bit cold from that moment on. My relationship with the account director was never fully repaired and would present a challenge that I never counted on down the line.

The next few months were a frenzy of meetings, advertising, packaging, and marketing materials for all the new mouse products that had to be ready in time for the targeted April launch. In early spring, Nancy had asked me to take on a small internal project for the finance department.

I did a few small projects leveraging the internal creative team to inform employees of some updates or changes that would affect everyone. This project was to educate employees about a stock split. I agreed to take it on and met with the designated finance person to gather input.

The finance person explained the information required in the communication for a publicly traded stock, and that the result was that every share of company stock would double on April 16, 1990. It was a significant benefit as the stock value would likely continue to increase following April 16. The guy was very excited and asked why I was so calm about this fantastic news. I told him that I had no experience with stock and didn't think it applied to me. He laughed, saying that this would affect all employees. Except, I had never heard anything about stock options.

After the meeting, I stopped by Nancy's office to let her know I had started the project. Before I left, I got up the nerve to ask her if I had stock. There had been no mention of it in my offer letter. She shook her head and pulled my paperwork out of her desk drawer. She confirmed that there was no mention of stock in my offer letter. She jumped up and told me to follow her. We walked straight into the company treasurer's office. Nancy introduced me and explained that we were there to check on the number of shares I had been awarded when hired. He looked it up and gave us the number of shares. I was not a significant shareholder, but I had skin in the game. The small project took on new meaning and importance once I knew how much it meant to me.

The computer industry was moving quickly, and the anticipation around a new innovative operating system from Microsoft was huge. The hardware business unit that I was working with was in the eye of the storm. The new operating system depended on a mouse to make it work. This software was going to change the way people worked with computers. It seemed like a stretch, but Windows 3.0 was a giant step toward making "a computer on every desk and in every home" a reality. PC manufacturers were already developing smaller, faster, more portable models, with the "Graphic User Interface" (GUI) that leveraged a mouse, and the hardware team was testing mobile versions that would become the "Ballpoint Mouse." Mice or touchpads were not built into computers at the time. The "Ballpoint Mouse" was the external hardware that would mount on the side of a laptop computer, much like an external camera.

The company was continually reorganizing, and I found myself with a new manager. Mark was a typical Microsoft employee: intense, smart, not afraid to take risks, and had his employees' backs. He was a few years older than me with a wife and a new baby. He worked long hours and expected a lot but had a friendly way about him and was always willing to be a sounding board or support a point of view if you had the information to back it up.

Mark was well liked by the hardware business leadership and, by all accounts, a part of the "in" club at the company. Mark wasn't from an agency and was very aware of the run-in I'd had with the agency team early on. He made it clear he approved of my willingness to do the right thing for the business and client.

Mark was savvy about navigating the corporate world, and during our first official one-on-one, he gave me a list of ten people at the company he recommended that I set up meetings with and get to know. I did it and credited those initial meetings with much of my success for years to come. The names on that list represented people at all levels across several business units. Every one of them accepted my invitation and sat down for a discussion.

Microsoft was growing fast, but there was a culture of collaboration and the feeling that it took everyone's contribution to move the business forward. You were expected to perform at the top of your game, but there were no restrictions on success. Or, if there were, I was never aware of them and simply moved forward with the expectation that I would continue to succeed.

The Announcement!

In early spring, I worked with the hardware team to develop a consumer testing plan for the new portable mouse that would be released several months after Windows 3.0 to expand the Microsoft hardware product line. The research plan included focus groups in the Bay area, so we planned to fly down in the afternoon, observe groups in the evening, and be back in the office by early afternoon the following day, Good Friday, 1990. The outcome of these groups would provide critical insight, so the Business Unit Manager (BUM) joined us for the trip.

At the airport Friday morning, the BUM went to pick up an *InfoWorld* magazine in the gift shop to read on the flight to Seattle. He came back to the group, sat down, and started flipping through the magazine. He stopped suddenly and stared down at a two-page ad featuring the new Microsoft Mouse in full color. It was a beautiful advertisement that showed off the sleek lines of the new mouse. This was the advertising that had defined my first few weeks at the company. I was responsible for it and proud of the creative and media plans I had approved. There was just one problem. The new Microsoft Mouse was being announced and released in coordination with the new operating system, Windows 3.0, and that announcement had been moved several times within the past thirty days. The latest date was for May 22, 1990. He was holding the April 16 edition of *InfoWorld*! He slowly held up the magazine so we could all see the beautiful full-color double-page advertisement. I was speechless. This was my fault.

My head immediately started to spin, and I thought I would throw up. I was responsible for that ad, and it was my first project at Microsoft. I had worked on every aspect of it, including the messaging strategy and the media plans. I had even traveled to New York for the photo shoot. Media plans were done months in advance of the actual advertisement showing up in a publication, and because the launch of Windows 3.0 had been a moving target, there had been several revisions to the media start dates. The explanation of how it happened didn't matter. The fact was that it was painfully clear that I had missed a publication change date somewhere along the way, and the result was that I had inadvertently advertised Microsoft's most significant product release in history to the world five weeks before the official product announcement.

The trip back was painful. My head was throbbing, trying to come up with a mitigation plan. The first thing was to ensure that the ad was only running in one publication and to contact the publisher and pull the remaining ads scheduled to appear between the issue that was out on newsstands and May 22. It sounded good until I realized that it was Good Friday, and all the publishers were closed for the holiday weekend.

The next order of business was to develop communications that would be used by our large phone-based inside sales organization and product support teams to respond when customers called in to ask where they could buy Windows 3.0 with the new Microsoft Mouse bundle they saw advertised.

There was a long list of internal and external people that were all gearing up for an enormous launch that needed to be told of the early advertisement. Large retailers had invested in promotions, had purchased product stock, and counted on the marketing efforts that Microsoft had committed to drive sales in their stores five weeks out.

I sat in my office until late in the evening, drafting emails on how to handle a customer inquiry, what to say to a partner that was outraged with no inventory to sell. My phone rang with calls from field salespeople asking what to say to their customers. Other CorpCom people stopped by my office to see if the rumors were true. Had I advertised Windows 3.0 before the announcement?

I called Doug to briefly explain that my career at Microsoft had been fantastic although short and that I would be very late coming home. I believed I would be fired once a communication plan was in place.

Mark was supportive and helped draft the checklist of who needed to be told but gave me space to do the heavy lifting and take responsibility.

On the list to receive communication was the Windows Business Unit Manager, Steve Ballmer. The stories of his boisterous personality were true; he was terrifying! I sent him an email explaining that I had announced the most significant product launch in the company's young history several weeks before the official release announcement. I included a list of all the things I was doing to ensure that our internal and external facing employees were aware of this issue and the things I was doing to ensure this type of thing would never happen again. All this communication was typed on a "dumb terminal" with single-line editing. In real terms, this meant that I had to type a line at a time and ensure it was correct before hitting the return key. The email took hours to write. Sure I would be fired, I started packing up my office and grabbed the suitcase from the trip to San Francisco that now seemed like it had been weeks before. It was well after 9:00 p.m. As I was ready to walk out the door, I received a reply from Steve B. "Understood" was all it said.

I went into work early Monday morning and was relieved when my card key still worked. Val, the department director, had been out of the office on Friday; however, I was very sure she was well versed on the issue by Monday. I heard her coming down the hall toward my office. As I looked up, she was standing in front of my desk holding the April 16, 1990, edition of *InfoWorld* open with the ad facing toward me. She didn't say a word. I stood up as calmly as I could and began to explain the communication plan that was already being executed. "Don't ever let something like this happen again," was all she said as she turned around and walked out of my office.

The next thing I heard about the significant gaffe on the mouse and Windows was in a column from a watchdog journalist noting that "Microsoft was not confirming the release of Windows 3.0 but one of their employees had saved them the trouble and cost of an announcement event by leaking the product in a full-color, double-page spread."

The remarkable thing about those few days that will stay with me in slow motion forever was that I kept my job; there was never another word said about it internally.

I took away a valuable lesson from that experience. Microsoft leadership was young, hungry, and aggressive. But they understood that people make mistakes and that, if you give them the opportunity, most competent people will recover, repair, and learn quickly. Continuing to drag people and issues through the mud serves little purpose beyond distracting the team. I have thought of this often, working with leaders who didn't share the organizational maturity that Microsoft's early group of leaders showed.

For my part, as severely shaken as I was, I had to choose how I would move forward. I could let the embarrassment of such a highly visible and public mistake get the best of me. However, I knew that I had done everything I could to take responsibility and fix the error, so I moved on.

THE WINDOWS 3.0 launch was a hit despite my blunder, and the company took off. We were growing and changing every day and suffered from growing pains. Each Monday was an adventure to get into the office to see if there had been a reorg planned over the weekend that would mean a new client business or manager. The joke around the company was that you always kept a stack of boxes in your office because we moved around so often you had to be ready. The employee base was growing at a breakneck pace. The release of Windows 3.0 was fueling massive growth in the computer industry. It ushered in a new way of working that depended on developers using it to build products that worked on Microsoft Windows. Bill was talking about "a computer in every office and every home," and it was becoming viable. It was a heady time.

One afternoon, not long after I moved into a window office with a view of the fountain in a central courtyard between buildings 8 and 9, trucks started showing up setting up tents, and bringing in hundreds of boxes of pizza and cases and cases of beer. Teams of people quickly built a temporary stage, and we received an email from Bill G, announcing Windows 3.0 had sold over 100,000 copies, and he wanted to celebrate. It was an all-company, impromptu party. I look back on these moments and smile, remembering how hard we worked and how many hours we spent on a mission to make Microsoft successful. A pop-up pizza and beer party was just the thing to keep everyone going.

As part of this extraordinary growth in resources, there were changes in leaders. The company was outgrowing some of the original talents that had been essential contributors in the early days. The level of business sophistication had increased dramatically. Val was one of those casualties, leaving the company a year after I joined. Her replacement was none other than the agency account director I had encountered on the mouse advertisement project during my first week at the company. It made for an uncomfortable situation. Since our first rocky engagement, I had steered clear, but he was now my boss. To make matters even worse, my office was next door to Val's— i.e., his—office. The announcement of the change in CorpCom leadership came out a few weeks before I was going on maternity leave and gave me time to make a game plan for when I returned that didn't include working for him.

Getting into the Business

When I returned from maternity leave, I was ready to make a change, so I began to look for open positions within the company and leveraged meetings with the original list of people that Mark had given to me when I first started. One man on the list, Mike, was responsible for developing the Microsoft product distribution channel. Microsoft products were sold in boxes on floppy disks. It required tremendous logistics to get those packages from a manufacturing plant north of Redmond, Washington, to store shelves across the United States and around the world. Mike was the man for the job. He came from the record business and was no stranger to the complexity and volatility of packaged product distribution. He was loud, brash, swore constantly, and was one of the smartest people I had ever met. Mike never sugarcoated anything. I witnessed many conversations with him telling product managers at the top of his lungs that their distribution or product was ridiculous, and they were stupid for thinking it would be attractive to a reseller. I was on the receiving end of a mock-up box for the Microsoft Mouse retail product that Mike hurled across a conference room table in response to a proposed special pricing promotion. I didn't take his action personally, and the behavior was acceptable at the time.

I enjoyed periodic lunches with Mike for over a year as a friendship was starting. He mentioned that the manager of the marketing team responsible for communicating distribution policies to partners was taking a new position and asked if I was interested in the job. I jumped at the opportunity. Leveraging an established relationship with a coworker to learn something new was a great way to move my career forward.

> Leveraging an established relationship with a coworker to learn something new was a great way to move my career forward.

I landed the new job, moved to a new building with a new manager, and for the first time, had a small team to manage. The new group was a bespoke team that reported into the sales organization. I was responsible for communicating the terms and conditions of the relationship with Microsoft to the partners.

At the time, over 85 percent of Microsoft revenue came from the partner channel, and we were highly dependent on collaboration with industry-leading partners to stock, market, and sell our products. My team and I became the conduit between the Microsoft account managers, the partners' leadership in the home markets, and Microsoft executives.

It was in this position that I learned some key lessons of people management. When I started in the job, my team consisted of three persons: me as the manager and two other women. One was responsible for the communication of partner terms and targets, and the other evaluated marketing plans and managed a co-op marketing compliance agency. Both of these women were tight with my predecessor, so neither was thrilled with the idea of a new manager.

I immediately ran into my first leadership challenge. One of my team members went on medical leave for a persistent back problem.

As a veteran of an orthopedic injury, I was supportive and knew that the company had a generous short-term disability policy. It was a busy time. We were rolling out semester programs, so having a significant part of the team absent had an impact and increased the workload on the two of us. Two weeks later, my remaining employee announced her decision to leave the company. Almost at the same moment, there was a reorganization in the sales division, and I had a new manager.

All of this was playing out as Doug and I were struggling with finding stable, affordable day care for our son Zach and juggling travel schedules. It was not uncommon for us to meet at the airport to exchange the baby.

I had photo shoots for two and three days and Doug traveled to the East Coast often, so he would leave the day I scheduled to arrive home. We made sure to sync our flights so that there would be an overlap at the airport. He met me at the arrival gate, and after a quick "How was your trip?" exchange, he handed over Zach, his diaper bag, the car keys, and a ticket for the airport parking. Kissed us both goodbye and disappeared down the corridor toward his gate. Time together as a family was precious, and even these quick reunions were important for continuity and connection.

On average days I would take the early shift at work, leaving the house between 6:00 a.m. and 6:30 a.m., then leaving the office by 5:00 p.m. to get across the Lake Washington bridge to pick up Zach before day care closed at 5:30 p.m. Doug would handle the morning drop-off and work until 7:00 p.m. or 8:00 p.m. each night. Our lives were crazy, but not unlike many young families with demanding careers.

With a short staff in the office, I had to step up and come up with a solution quickly. The first order of business was to assess the workload left by two vacant positions in my team and come up with a plan to get it out the door. There was no option to backfill for medical leave, and I was determined to hire for the long term for the other open position.

My new manager, Sharon, was a well-respected longtime Microsoft employee. Sharon was in her late forties with grown children. Nothing rattled her, and she had a wicked sense of humor. Our first conversation was something like, "Great to meet you. I have a team of two people; one is on disability and one quit yesterday." She responded by pointing out that I had no time to talk to her and that I should get the hell out of her office and get to work hiring for my open position. She made it very clear that she had my back and was there to support me. Sharon was one of those extraordinary people you come across in business that are fun, insightful, and *bold*.

The Microsoft culture was evolving but embraced some unique management styles that were essential to keeping employees engaged as the company grew exponentially. I was fortunate enough to have one of those managers in Sharon with an unusual style that taught me a lot about managing and supporting teams. Calling Sharon an unconventional manager was an understatement. Before taking on our group, she managed the Inside Sales team of five hundred employees. Sharon moved into an office just off the elevators in the center of a long hall of Sales Support offices. She brought along a dorm-sized refrigerator and established 6:00 p.m. happy hour on Fridays and any other day that was challenging or needed to be celebrated. The fridge was stocked with cheap white wine, and the team managed to find snacks to accompany whenever required.

If the day was particularly bad, Sharon would stroll down the corridor clutching her briefcase to her chest. We quickly learned it was code for a scotch day. The briefcase housing a bottle of blended scotch only left her office as a signal that happy hour was starting. From the day Sharon took over my team, my office supplies included a corkscrew, plastic cups, and cocktail napkins. Sharon became one of my biggest advocates. I learned the value and process of building relationships with your teams from her that I took forward and leveraged throughout my career.

The company and the field sales forces were growing like crazy. To keep up with this demand, I was asked to develop a new discipline of Field Marketing. The idea was to staff the field offices with marketing execution resources to manage local campaigns and events, all reporting to a leader on my team. Adding a Field Marketing area to my scope was a fantastic opportunity for me to grow my team, increase my visibility, and continue climbing the corporate ladder.

Lessons

1. Interviewing is tricky. Being prepared, in my mind, is understanding what you are looking for in a position and an employer and being ready for a discussion—not simply having canned answers that the employer will expect and is getting from every other candidate. You are considering spending lots of time and energy for this company, so make sure you feel comfortable having honest conversations and that you can be yourself.

2. People make mistakes. Acknowledging the mistake and moving forward will facilitate recovery. Continuing to review a mistake will destroy a team or project every time.

3. People management is an art. Understanding who the people are and what their relationships are is as critical as the job they perform. Leading people is much easier when they are motivated to follow.

seven

If He Can Do It

N THE SPRING OF 1993, I heard from one of my CorpCom friends that my former boss in CorpCom, Mike, was moving to Paris to take a job in the European HQ. This was the same guy I met early on in my Microsoft career as the agency account director. The first thought that came to mind was, "If he can do that, why can't I?" Mike was part of the boys' club at the company. Having worked with him as an external vendor, then for him internally, I was less than impressed. I couldn't let go of the feeling that I was just as smart and ambitious, so why was I not moving to Paris? The time that Doug and I spent in Thailand just after we were married made an enormous impression on us both. When we first returned to the States, we talked about finding a way to move overseas again and figured that since he was working for a Japanese company, that would be the likely path. When the email announcement came out about Mike's promotion, it changed everything for me.

My career was moving forward. I was earning a good salary, but in the back of my mind, this was not the life I wanted to build. I never had the idyllical middle-class life before, so this was all new. The lifestyle I had was what young professionals all over the country were striving for. Couples would marry, buy a house, spend money on cars, restaurants, and expensive toys for a few years. Once the baby came, the wife would stay home and create the picture-perfect suburban house for her family. That was what every TV show represented as success—but I wanted an adventure and a career like Mike was embarking on in Paris. Reading the email announcement struck a chord in me. I wanted to try new things, meet new people, take on more responsibility at work. I was willing to disrupt the steady life I had to achieve that goal. I knew that pursuing this ambition would be going against the grain. My friends all thought it ridiculous to give up the "perfect" life I was establishing. Women didn't consider this type of global career as an option. It never occurred to me that I couldn't do it.

During my next one-on-one with Sharon, I shared my career goal to work in a subsidiary office. In true Sharon style, she shook her head and said that I was completely nuts, but she followed up quickly with a promise of her full support. I was ecstatic and felt like the world was suddenly open with endless possibilities.

> I was estatic and felt like the world was suddenly open with endless possibilities.

I was impatient to get my intention to a broader audience, so I went back to the list of influential people that Mark had given me and set up coffee meetings to share my ambition of working in an overseas office. As a result of those conversations, I was introduced to people working in subsidiaries all over the world and started having phone calls and meetings with them when they visited corporate HQ to learn about their jobs.

Their first question was always, "Why the interest in working internationally?" My response always centered around increasing my knowledge of the business and scope of responsibility. I never mentioned that a guy I knew was moving to Paris, and I figured I could do the same. It didn't take long for the news to spread.

As demand for Microsoft products grew in the market, so did our sales force and the need for support from my team to provide even more on-the-ground marketing resources. My group got four new people and more responsibility.

One of my new team members was Jan. Jan had been on the client side for a project I had done during my time in CorpCom. She was a terrible client, condescending and unkind to me throughout the project. Our encounter stands out to me as one of the worst experiences I had working with client teams at the company. She now reported to me, which could have ended in a disastrous situation.

As a standard practice, I met with all my new employees within the first few days of their joining my team. I used these meetings to get to know the new person and provide them with insight on how I viewed their function fitting into the team's mission, and to encourage them to share their career aspirations and their working style. This occasion presented a unique situation for me and an opportunity to hone my management and leadership skills.

When Jan arrived in my office, she was ready with defenses up and almost immediately launched into a speech about how she assumed that I would use this situation to treat her as poorly as she had treated me on our first encounter. I let her have her say and then explained that that was not my approach. To make the transition to the team, we would need to make a fresh start. She was shocked but agreed to give it a try. The encounter with Jan was one of the most important leadership lessons I learned in my early career at Microsoft. Jan and I found a rhythm and she worked on my team until I moved overseas.

The company needed to scale, so the focus was on putting people in positions where they could be most effective, regardless of their age, where they went to school, or how senior their previous role was. When managing this level of explosive growth, the business had to leverage talent wherever it was needed. The tool of choice was reorganization. They happened so regularly that we joked about the game the whole company could play: Who is your manager today and what group do you work in? It was standard practice to keep a box in your office to be ready to move to your new team. You never wanted to burn a bridge because you could end up working for that person.

A casualty of the frequent reorganizations was Jack. He was British, quirky, and abrasive by American standards. He said whatever came to mind with little filter or concern for his audience. He had worked in technology in the UK and had come to Redmond via the South African subsidiary, where he landed on the US Channel Marketing team. I didn't know it then, but Jack would figure prominently in my career for the next several years. I had worked with him on a few projects and was not surprised that he had only lasted a short time on a US-focused team. He was smart and had in-depth knowledge of the partner channel, but because of his lack of sensitivity, he was very unpopular with his American colleagues and customers.

Jack reached out to have lunch with me a few months after I started sharing my plans. His new role was on the headquarters-based team supporting the Africa, India, and Middle East (AIME) subsidiaries. Jack's specific responsibility was to support marketing for that group of countries. He heard that I was interested in working internationally, and there was an open role for a marketing manager position based in Dubai with responsibility across the Middle Eastern countries that I might be interested in. I had no idea where Dubai was. The Middle East had not been among the assignments that I had dreamed of for my field adventure.

> The Middle East had not been among the assignments that I had dreamed of for my field adventure.

I imagined living as an expatriate in Europe or Australia. These were places that business was growing, and I had met people from those offices when they came to Redmond. Their lives and jobs sounded exciting but manageable. The only thing I knew about the Middle East is that the first Gulf War (Desert Storm) was wrapping up, and oilfields that we depended on to put gas in our cars were on fire in the deserts of Kuwait. My Middle East facts didn't include any information about a place called Dubai, but I knew that culturally this was not an ideal place for a woman to work, much less expect career advancement. I thanked Jack for lunch and told him I would need to think about it and went back to my office. I looked Dubai up on a world map when I got home and mentioned the lunch and the opportunity almost in passing to Doug that evening. There was no way this seemed reasonable.

Several days later, I got another email from Jack asking if I had given the job in Dubai any more thought. As I was reading the email, I thought, *What the heck; it won't hurt to find out more*, so I responded that I wanted additional details and to meet some of the other AIME Redmond-based team. Jack set up a meeting with his boss, Bryan and the subsidiary liaison, Tanya, for the following week.

It was midsummer. Seattle was beautiful. I walked over to the building where Bryan, Jack, and Tanya's offices were, not knowing what to expect but excited at the possibilities. Even if this wasn't the right fit, the fact that I had the opportunity to meet the team and start the interview process solidified that this plan had potential. Bryan was seemingly a typical Microsoft guy, mid-thirties, good-looking, and charming. Tanya, the subsidiary liaison, provided a grounded view of the subsidiary challenges and shared how she supported and represented the field office at corporate. The meetings ended with an invitation for Doug and me to travel to Dubai and have a look around along with a VHS promotional video about Dubai entitled *Back in Dubai*. The theme music is still running through my head as I type.

The first time I had mentioned Dubai to Doug, there was no formal process or next steps. Now we had been invited to go and have a look at the job and the lifestyle in Dubai. I presented the idea over dinner as a chance for exploration. The job, if I even got it, was only a two-year contract and would be like an extended vacation for him. It would give him the chance to spend more time with Zach, and we could travel to interesting places for holidays. It was a long shot all the way around, but at the very least, Microsoft was paying for us to have a short vacation together. He agreed to go on the trip.

"Back in Dubai"

There is a twelve-hour time difference between Dubai and Seattle. After a short phone call in the middle of the night with the Middle East General Manager, Chuck, Doug and I were booked on British Airways for a five-day visit to Dubai. We shared the news with a few friends and enlisted Carrie and her husband to stay with Zach. We learned that our next-door neighbors had a connection to a young family—Matt and Susan—from Idaho that was working in Dubai for Caterpillar. We had a phone call with Matt as soon as our travel dates were confirmed and arranged to spend an evening with him and his wife in the hopes of gaining some outside perspective on life with a family and small child in this very foreign land.

There were few flights to Dubai in those days, so our route required an overnight stay in London. This was a bonus since neither of us had been to Europe. It was mid-August, but London was damp and chilly. We wandered around Piccadilly Circus, drank warm beer with fish and chips, and quickly became so tired we barely made it back to our airport hotel and fell into bed.

The following day was another seven-hour flight that landed late at night in Dubai. It was dark, so we saw nothing on the approach. As we stood in the aisle waiting to deplane, we assumed that the sudden overwhelming heat that filled the cabin was because the door was close to the engines. As we stepped onto the stairs, the rush of heavy, wet air turned out to be our first taste of Dubai in the summer. By the time we exited the airport, it was well past midnight, yet the city was alive. As we drove to the hotel in the taxi, we passed volleyball games and children playing in the park as if it were mid-day. The hotel clerk told us that it was too hot during the day for most activities, so during the warm months, activities were shifted to nighttime. The standard workday was from approximately 9:30 to 13:00 and in the evening from 16:00 to 19:00. Prime dinner time was 22:00 (10:00 p.m.), so what we were seeing was after-work, evening activities. The workweek in Dubai was also different. It started on Sunday and ended midday Thursday; the twenty-four-hour clock added to the strange feeling. *Nothing* was familiar.

I arranged to meet Chuck, the Middle East General Manager, in the lobby of the Hilton Hotel (where we were staying) the next morning. He arrived and explained that I would be going to the office with him, and someone would be by shortly to collect Doug and take him on his day of sightseeing. Chuck was an odd guy, and it was clear that our potential situation of a wife working to support the family while the husband stayed home with the children was not common—especially in this part of the world in 1993. The local office had no idea what to do with Doug while I was looking into the business.

Travel to Dubai took two days. We had meetings and tours scheduled for two days, then a flight home at 3:00 a.m. on the third night. Time was short, and we had a lot to take in and discuss.

I went to the office and met the Middle East team the first morning. It was an eclectic group of about twenty people from fourteen different nations; some of their home countries I would be hard-pressed to find on a map. We quickly found common ground in the shared passion for Microsoft products and how they could change the world. The team was fascinating. I was excited by the challenge of the emerging markets, and all I could learn and experience with these people.

Doug spent the day with a friend of a friend from the office. He visited stores, villas (houses for rent), and shopping malls. We met back at the hotel, exhausted and jet-lagged, to share our adventures of the day. I started with, "I think we could do this," barely taking a breath before launching into the fantastic team of people from all corners of the world, the opportunity in the market, and so on. Doug listened quietly. He began with, "We could never do this." It was crazy foreign, expensive, and he didn't like malls or shopping. We had a quick dinner and collapsed in bed, each trying to sort out the other's perspective during a restless night.

The next day, I returned to the office for more meetings, this time with local and regional partners. These meetings provided an entirely different perspective. Customer service was not a focus, and partners had little interest in the business but enjoyed the notoriety that came from leveraging the Microsoft brand with their company name. Business deals were done very differently and would be painful to evolve to Western business practices.

A Microsoft partner named Sonja took Doug around to see schools and shops located in the neighborhood where the Western expatriates lived. Sonja was German and had been married to a member of the UAE Royal Family. She spoke five languages and knew everything and everyone in Dubai and the UAE.

We arranged to have dinner with Matt and Susan, the American family working for Caterpillar, that night in the hopes of getting a perspective on life in this desert. Doug and I arrived at the hotel about the same time and quickly changed for dinner. I started my top-line analysis of the day with, "There is no way I can do this . . ." Doug followed soon with, "After today, I think we can do this."

We went to dinner at Matt and Susan's villa. They would become the central point of contact into the expat community living in the Jamaira area of Dubai (and have remained some of our dearest friends). They had a little girl a year older than Zach and lived in a compound of beautiful California-style homes with outdoor space, built-in pools, and live-in maids. We had a fantastic evening and knew that if we could agree on a compensation package, we had found friends. We returned to the hotel and spent long hours in the night creating a spreadsheet outlining the compensation package we needed to make a move.

The third day started with a meeting with Chuck, followed by a call with Bryan to share my expectations of a compensation package. I spent the rest of the day meeting with other people in the subsidiary. Chuck planned a dinner at the hotel late in the evening, and then we would head directly to the airport for our flight home via London. Nothing more was mentioned about the elements of compensation I had asked for or a formal offer for the rest of the day.

Once back at the hotel, Chuck and I took the two empty seats at the long table in the dining room where Doug and several of the people from the office, partners, and vendors we had met during the trip were already seated. About an hour into the meal, the hotel manager approached me to let me know I had a phone call in his office. It was Bryan. There was some small talk about the visit and my impressions before he formally offered me the position as the Marketing Manager for the Middle East with all of the elements of my requested package plus a few thousand dollars more added to the salary. I accepted and headed back to the business table. Doug was seated at the other end of the table, so we had no opportunity to talk. At midnight, we wrapped up dinner, and Chuck drove us to the airport.

As we walked through the front doors of the airport to join the immigration queue, I told Doug that I had accepted the job and needed to be "back in Dubai" in three weeks to manage the Middle East version of the consumer electronics show GITEX (Gulf Information Technology Exhibition). He was quiet for a minute as our passports were stamped and handed back. To my relief, he took my hand and smiled and said, "We have a ton to do in a short time," as we walked to the gate area. In many ways, this was a repeat of the decision process we had made in going to Thailand—only at that time he was taking an opportunity, and we weren't married. This time, my decision would have implications for our marriage, child, and income. We were truly in it together.

Lessons

1. Make the time to build a network that is wide and strong before you need it. It will deliver value to your career and personal development. You will learn things you didn't even know you needed.

2. If there is something you want, go after it. Start from what you know and how you will be an asset to a job or situation and learn the rest on the way. Women frequently start from what they are qualified for instead of focusing on all of the attributes they bring.

3. If there is no specific rule, policy, or law that says you can't do something, do it. Just because it hasn't been done before doesn't mean it can't be done.

4. Be careful what you ask for. You might get it.

eight

I Took the Job

T O SAY THE NEXT THREE weeks flew by would be an understatement. Doug and I barely spoke on the flight to London—both lost in our thoughts about what this would all mean for our lives. By the time we started the final leg to Seattle, the decision had begun to settle in, and we jumped deep into planning mode. How would Zach take it? How would we tell our families? What about our friends? What would they say? For me, it started with the reality of taking this job and asking Doug to stay home with Zach. I was taking on 100 percent responsibility for supporting our family. *Shit!*

I gave Sharon official notice that I was leaving my first day back in the office. I met with Microsoft legal counsel about my contract, with the tax people on the implications of a salary in foreign currency, and with a variety of other HR people. The process was not smooth. Microsoft had moved people to Paris, the UK, Australia, and even one to South Africa. However, I was the first going to the Middle East, and only the thirtieth person overall to leave the corporate office for a subsidiary job. Plus, there was an additional complexity of moving to the United Arab Emirates. The UAE doesn't have an income tax system, the currency was calibrated to the US dollar, and there was no such thing as a standard company expatriate package. All of this meant that my meetings with corporate representatives were short and most often turned into a conversation on how I wanted to handle things rather than them providing guidance or laying out terms of my package. We learned together.

I planned to leave Seattle in three weeks. My head was already in Dubai, ready to manage the GITEX event, meet the partners, get to know a little about the Middle East market, and find a place for us to live. Doug would leave his job as soon as possible and would be the point person for all the relocation people, would rent our house, and would tie up our personal business. My employment contract was for two years, with no guarantee of a job when I returned. It did give us pause; however, by this time, we were swept up in the adventure, so we decided that finding a position to come home to would be a project to focus on down the line.

The week before I left Seattle, I celebrated my thirtieth birthday—a milestone of maturity. I was embarking on a new chapter of life that was scary but exhilarating. My departure day was full of emotion: terrifying, sad, and exciting. I had now traveled out of the country three times, but this time I was alone. I was leaving my husband and precious baby for a month. I had no idea what to expect or how I should be feeling.

On some level, I felt overwhelming guilt for leaving my family. Everyone I knew told me how crazy this was and how taking this job would ruin my marriage and my relationship with my child. I have to be honest. I was petrified that they might be right and that Zach would begin to prefer Doug over me as his primary caregiver, as his mom. I knew Doug and I would get through it but also suddenly felt the pressure of being 100 percent responsible for supporting my family. It was daunting and scary, but another part of me felt exhilarated and excited. It was right. This was precisely where I was supposed to be! They drove me to the airport and waited with me at the gate until it was time to board the flight to London.

The plane ride to London was uneventful, and I was in the British Airways lounge at Heathrow when the alarm went off throughout the airport. Terminal four was evacuated to the parking lot. There was no peace treaty with Northern Ireland yet, and there were regular security issues in the UK during this period. This particular day, an explosive device had been thrown over the fence and landed on a runway; airport officials were taking no chances. I moved with the rest of the passengers, wholly overwhelmed and terrified. The voice in my head kept repeating, "What have you done?"

| The voice in my head kept repeating, "What have you done?"

The trip continued several hours later without incident. I landed in the middle of the night and collected my bags. I was *not* an experienced traveler. Instead of a few large suitcases that could be loaded on a trolley and put easily into a taxi and a hotel room, I had five small bags of varying shapes and sizes. The first penalty was the extra bag charge from British Airways, followed by several trips to and from the bag carousel, the taxi, and into my hotel room.

After a restless first night, I pulled myself together and drove my rental car across the sand for my first day of work at the Microsoft Middle East office (Microsoft ME). I jumped in with both feet and both hands. The largest IT event in the region was taking place in three and a half weeks, and Microsoft ME had an enormous presence. To the team, I was the instant expert on all things Microsoft and marketing; it was overwhelming but fun. I worked on every aspect of the event, from media relationships and partner presentations to lighting in the booth and shopping for clothes for demo people to wear. It was fifteen-hour days, a decision every minute.

Sonja, the owner of our marketing agency that Doug and I had met on our first visit, became a friend and partner immediately. Sonja knew everyone in the business community and how to get things done in Dubai.

GITEX was a three-day annual event. The Middle East/Africa regional director, Bryan, and the Microsoft International VP, Chris, were both coming to the trade show, along with several other international guests coming to conduct partner meetings and technical presentations. I planned to return to Seattle two days after the trade show ended.

I spent the whole night before the event making sure everything was working and in order. I had just enough time to shower and change before greeting the international executives and partners as they streamed to our booth in the main hall of the exhibition center.

On the second day of the event, Microsoft ME hosted a meeting for all the regional partners so they could meet with the VP from Redmond. This meeting turned out to be the most important of my career in the Middle East. Microsoft and Bill Gates were already iconic: Bill was a visionary and our partners all wanted a piece of his rising star.

I was the only woman at the meeting in a room full of thirty-five Microsoft partners from more than twenty countries. The first thing that Chris did as he stood up to address the group about Microsoft strategy and business plans in the region was to introduce me. He gave them my name and title, then said that I was in the job to represent Bill Gates, and whatever I said was to be heard as the direction of Bill Gates, and they should respect me as they would him. Even though I was confident in my ability and felt secure in the position, the cultural norm was against me: Chris bridged the gap between my strength and self-confidence and perceived strength. I could not have asked for a better or more impactful start to my Middle Eastern journey. Chris had set the tone that would almost assure success for me in the region, and he was an ally and an example of how valuable support can be.

The evening following GITEX, my GM had arranged to have dinner with a few engineers who had come to show off the latest products, among them Peter and Mike. On the way to dinner, they asked if we could stop by the *souk* (market), so they could buy gifts before dinner. The Gold Souk was across Dubai Creek from the office in Deira. I had been there a few times and thought I could manage.

The mission started fine. We found a parking spot, and each of them purchased a gold necklace for their wives. The trip back to Dubai proved to be my undoing. We found our car, but the souk is an old market with narrow, winding streets that made it impossible for a novice to find the exit. Each time I thought I saw a path to the main road, I hit a dead end and had to back up down the narrow alley and try the next one. I drove in circles for over an hour until I was utterly beside myself with frustration and worry. My passengers were already very late for dinner, and it was my fault. I was trying so hard to make a good impression on my new boss, new team, and these guys from Redmond, and it was rapidly unraveling into incompetence. After another twenty minutes of driving in circles, Mike turned to me with a comment that I would use in many other situations in the years to come. He said, "Even if you are unsuccessful in your job in the Middle East, you already have enough stories for years of dinner parties." It was a brilliant observation, and the perspective I needed at that moment. Ultimately, I found our way out, I dropped them off in time for coffee and dessert, and I flew home the following day to pack Zach and Doug up and say goodbye to our family and friends.

The Goodbye Tour

I arrived in Seattle, exhausted and excited. I had completed the first small steps in my new job, and GITEX had been a success by all accounts. I had two weeks to get my life in order, bring my family to Dubai, and get back at work. The reunion was terrific at first, but within a few hours, it was clear that Zach was not adjusting well to all the changes in his young life. He was usually a happy, friendly toddler, but now he cried quickly. Whenever possible he made sure that he was touching me or sitting on my lap, but he wouldn't face me. He was confused and upset that I had been gone and didn't know how to manage his emotions at two years old. I felt terrible!

For the first time since he was a few days old, I slept in the same bed with him and took him everywhere with me. Zach's reaction was a challenge that I hadn't counted on and had no idea how to handle. After several days in Seattle, saying goodbye and packing up, we began the farewell tour. The first stop was to see my mother in Northern California, then Kansas to visit my aging grandmother, and finally Pittsburgh to see Doug's family and celebrate Thanksgiving. The trip was taxing and emotional. Zach was still upset. The Friday after Thanksgiving, the three of us were finally on the plane to London, and it sunk in: we were now expatriates.

IT SEEMED AS though we quickly fell into a rhythm in Dubai. I had colleagues at the office and had the benefit of having worked with them for a month before Doug and Zach arrived. Matt and Susan welcomed us into the Western expatriate community and quickly included us in all the social functions. Doug was a point of interest all around. The husbands couldn't get their heads around the fact that it was my job that had brought us to Dubai and not Doug's. The wives didn't know how to engage with a "stay-at-home dad."

Doug had no interest in the coffee mornings or afternoon shopping trips. He preferred finding activities to make sure the kids were busy. He got the moms to sign all the kids up for tennis, horseback riding, trips to the park, anything to ensure that Zach and several of his nursery schoolmates were busy. This was a completely new world for him in a number of ways. We had always shared chores around the house; however, we had fallen into the traditional husband and wife roles. I prepared most of the meals, did the shopping, and made sure Zach had clothes, shoes, and so on. That all changed in Dubai. Doug took over everything domestic. He saw all of this as another opportunity for adventure. Zach settled in, was swimming, and started ordering "iced lollies" within a few weeks.

What Are You Wearing to MYR?

Every January signified a key business event at Microsoft, Mid-Year Review. It was the midpoint in the fiscal year when the executives wanted to have a detailed discussion about your sales numbers, what was going well, and what was not working. It was the opportunity to forecast annual performance, share wins and losses, and ask for help. The business review revolved around a set of standard slides and spreadsheets that every subsidiary and business unit completed and presented during a two-to-four-hour meeting. The subsidiaries presented their deck to the respective regional directors. The regional directors then presented a summary deck to the area VP, and finally, it was rolled up and presented to Bill G. and the Office of the President, called the "BOOP" for short. This process happened twice a year, once at the midpoint and again at the start of the fiscal year, to present an Annual Business Plan.

In Redmond, I never had much to do with the Mid-Year Review; however, as the Middle East Marketing Manager, I was responsible for completing and presenting the standard deck in partnership with my general manager. The preparation meetings began as soon as the GITEX trade show finished. Our formal review meeting with the leadership team would take place in Johannesburg, South Africa, in the second week of January. Pulling the midyear business review data and plan together was crazy, but it was a fantastic way to learn my new job.

The deck was finally complete. We printed thirty copies, and the team agreed to meet in the airport lounge ahead of our 2:00 a.m. flight to Johannesburg. We were to arrive in the early afternoon the day before our meeting to allow time for a dry run. Six other subsidiaries from around our region were traveling to South Africa to have review meetings within a three-day window. I was nervous and excited about the trip. Apartheid was still in place, which made traveling to Johannesburg risky but very interesting. The business review meeting was an opportunity for me to show Bryan and Chris that they had made the right choice and that I was going to make a difference in the Middle East business.

I had arrived in Dubai just over a month before traveling to Johannesburg for the business review. There hadn't been time on either of my previous two trips to process my resident visa, so I was still entering the country using a single-entry tourist visa. At the time, many nationalities, including the United States, required a visa to enter the country for any reason.

I passed through the immigration line at the airport, handed over my visa, with my passport stamped that I had officially left the country. The paperwork was in place for a new single-entry visa upon my return in four days. There was one flight every four days between Dubai and Johannesburg. The flight delay announcement came just before we were to board, saying that, due to a mechanical issue, the flight had been rescheduled for the following morning. The team all decided to go home, get some sleep, and come back for the flight in the morning. Home sounded like a great idea, but it was not an option for me. I had no valid visa to reenter the country, so I slept in the lounge.

The airline had removed the bags from the plane the night before and required each passenger to recheck them the next morning. The flight time was eight hours between Dubai and Joburg, so we would now arrive late the night before our MYR meeting. After an hour at the baggage claim, all the luggage had arrived except for my suitcase. South African Airlines finally located it in Dubai and said they would have it on the next flight down in four days. The same flight we were booked on to return to Dubai. There was no sense in sending it. I had now been wearing and sleeping in my leggings and oversized shirt, designed to be the perfect travel clothes, for thirty-six hours. During Apartheid, stores in Joburg closed for the night at 5:00 p.m. and reopened again at nine the next morning. Our meeting was at 9:00 a.m.

We arrived at the hotel and explained the whole sordid tale to Bryan. After a chuckle, he welcomed me to the glamour of international business travel. There was an American woman who was working in the subsidiary as a product manager; he offered to call and see if she could help with my wardrobe. Her name was Kathy. We had met in Redmond a year before and didn't care for one another. But in this situation, when she knocked on my hotel room with three outfits, including clean underwear, she instantly became my best friend. The Mid-Year Review meeting went well, and we landed back in Dubai without further incident. I never saw the bag again. This was my second baggage incident, so from that moment on, I learned to travel light with only a carry-on bag containing an outfit that I could wear to any business function.

The Only Househusband in the Middle East—Jumeriah Jim

The visa and flight drama were only a part of the stress I felt during that first business review. Doug and I had gone out to dinner on the way to the airport. We were chatting about the new experiences we were having when Doug confided that he was miserable and that he thought we had made a terrible mistake by coming to Dubai. I was speechless. I knew that the adjustment he had made from working full-time to staying at home with the toddler was hard, amplified by the fact that he was virtually on his own in the role of a househusband in the community. But I hadn't counted on this level of dissatisfaction. I was very busy with my new job and only looked at the surface. He was so serious that I was worried and asked flat out if he and Zach would still be there when I got back. He answered, "I don't know." I had no idea how to deal with this but had a plane to catch. I went through the airport check-in and immigration in a daze, replaying the conversation over and over. Maybe everyone had been right, and this was a crazy move. Maybe I should have been happy with my "perfect" traditional life. I knew this would be hard, but I wasn't ready to give up my family for a job.

This was in the 1990s, so there was no such thing as a smartphone. There was no opportunity to talk for the next hour as I passed through security and immigration at the airport, and he drove home. Once in the airline lounge, I called home to talk. He immediately apologized for having been dramatic about his adjustment and told me that it had been a particularly hard day and he was tired of explaining his unique situation of being a "trailing spouse." While he had willingly taken on the househusband role, the reality was that he was bored. We had only been in Dubai for a little over a month as a family, so we didn't yet fully understand how to engage with the Western community other than the few social occasions we had attended. Doug had to reinvent himself without the benefit of a social structure to slip into. The exchanging of roles between us did not define our relationship, and we hadn't really stopped to consider the impact all of this would have. When people heard that my husband stayed home, the immediate assumption was either that he was weak or that I was a bitch that ordered him around. Nothing could have been further from the truth. Doug and I are equals, strong-willed, and both like to be in charge. Now we were in charge of different things and needed to pause and process this. We were aware that, along with the list of positives that carving out a unique lifestyle would bring to our family, there would also be challenges. Doug was suddenly overwhelmed with managing all of these changes. During the phone conversation in the airport lounge that evening, we had a long, honest discussion and agreed to lock arms and navigate this new world together.

To make matters worse for Doug's adjustment, as a woman, I was not allowed to sponsor a family for a resident visa. The consequence was that Doug and Zach were in the UAE on sixty-day tourist visas for the first nine months. At the end of each sixty days, they would fly to Bahrain and stay at a hotel for three days while their new tourist visa was processed. Microsoft picked up the tab, but it was very disruptive. In the end, the only way around it was for Microsoft to extend employment to Doug with a $0 salary that gave him the ability under UAE law to sponsor a family in the country.

Lessons

1. The unexpected will happen when traveling. Be ready and be flexible. Don't let it derail your trip. Be comfortable but aware. Assess the situation and act thoughtfully.

2. When traveling internationally, fewer, larger bags is a winning strategy!

3. Communication is everything. Work is necessary; however, if you are not sensitive and listening to the people you care most about, you may lose them.

nine

A New Business Model

FOLLOWING THE APPROVAL OF THE Mid-Year Plan, I started traveling across the Middle East region to get to know the partners, customers, and see their markets firsthand. The first order of business was to change the way products were distributed in the region. This change would reduce the margins for partners significantly and allow for more competitive pricing. But, it was a new way of doing business in the area, and this change (or any change) wasn't exactly welcome.

The introduction of competitive distribution was a long-term change that was not popular with the partners. The response was shock, disbelief, and anger—in that order. It made matters worse that news of the change was coming from a woman. Few of our partners had experience working with a woman at this level.

Some of the men gave me the cold shoulder upon hearing the news of the intent to change the current business practice. Some refused to talk or look at me and walked out of meetings. One even climbed on the table between us and screamed, "You are completely crazy if you think this is how to do business in the Middle East!" But, by the end of my second year in Dubai, I had signed a deal with Computer 2000, the largest hardware and software distributor in Europe, and they were doing business in three key markets in the region. To get to that point, I had traveled thousands of miles, met with every managing partner, and endured an assortment of reactions.

I received weekly gifts from that man for months to apologize for his behavior. Change was difficult, but it was possible because, in the end, we were able to communicate the benefit for both sides.

Arabic Wedding Wishes

My travel in the region gave me insight into just how rich and diverse the cultures of the Middle Eastern countries are and how warm the people can be. I became friends with Abdalla, our Business Development Manager, based in Amman. Abdalla had a calm, steady way about him. He had grown up in Jordan, went to university in the United States, and returned home to marry his cousin, as was the custom. He moved fluidly between Arab and American language and culture and was a patient teacher for me.

Air travel to some countries in the region was difficult for Americans. The first Gulf War had ended less than three years earlier, and America's role was not viewed as positive by all. Traveling by car was the preferred method into Lebanon and Syria because the border crossings were more discreet and accessible for Americans. However, it still involved the complexity of multiple vehicles. The first hired car took us from Amman to the border crossing between Jordan and Syria and passed through several checkpoints that began a few miles from the border on the Jordan side. In addition to meetings with government officials in Damascus, we were delivering a satellite antenna to our distribution partner. Equipment like the antenna that enabled unchecked international communication was against the law in Syria. This car was equipped with "special compartments" that held my PC and the satellite antenna to ensure they got across the border undetected. The second vehicle was contracted just over the border on the Syria side and took us to the outskirts of Damascus. Finally, the third vehicle was a city taxi, a Russian-made Trabant 601—basically a small square box.

At each checkpoint, when the guard discovered I was American and worked for Microsoft, a tariff was imposed and to be paid with a souvenir with the Microsoft logo on it. These ranged from mousepads to ink pens.

All passengers were required to enter the customs and immigration building to have their passport and visa stamped by an immigration officer when crossing the border. We carried our luggage (except the electronics safely stowed in the hidden compartment) into the building. As I walked through the door, all conversation stopped. Abdalla instructed me to approach the window; it felt like the parting of the Red Sea. The crowd of men moved away, clearing a path for me. I slid my passport to the officer behind the window. He grabbed it and, with a stone face, motioned for me to back up. Backing away from the counter and leaving my passport with a bored official felt uncomfortable and wrong, but I had no choice. A few windows down, another officer was sitting behind a desk, stamping passports. Each time he stamped one, he called out a name and, without looking up, tossed the passport over the barrier into the waiting crowd. There was a short scramble and the owner of the passport emerged victorious with his passport and hastily exited the building to continue his journey. This scene was repeated over the next thirty minutes while I waited for our passports to be tossed over the barrier. When my name was called, my passport was launched through the air as the others had been, but this time a hush fell over the building occupants, and again, a path was made for me to collect my passport off the floor of the lobby. We waited a few more minutes for Abdalla to go through the same process and were both relieved to be on our way.

Following successful customer meetings, the delivery of smuggled equipment to our partner, and dinner at the Marriott Damascus, Abdalla and I passed a banquet room where a wedding celebration was in full swing. Arabic weddings have separate ceremonies for the bride and groom; this one was for the bride. Abdalla had the idea that attending this celebration would give me some additional insight into Arab culture, so he asked a woman entering the room if the bride would mind if I joined in. Within minutes, she and two other women emerged from the ballroom, took me by the hands, and escorted me in to meet the bride and join in the fun.

It was a memorable experience, and one of the most remarkable evenings I had in the Middle East. All of the participants were joyfully dancing, talking, and laughing. This was a side of the life of Arabic women that is rarely seen or talked about. I was surrounded by women who were close, loving, and happy. I spent 98 percent of my time in the region dealing with Arabic men talking business. It felt special to be welcomed into this very female ritual. I made it to my room several hours and one henna tattoo later.

"I Will Take You Down"

After two years, my contract was coming to an end, and it was time to start planning my next move. I had learned about doing business in emerging economies, and how to work with men in a cultural context where women were not common in professional positions. I had amazing experiences. I felt that it was time to move to a more significant market, with more responsibility.

We were settled into international life. Doug had found his footing and was enjoying life, focusing on the family. He agreed that we wanted to continue living abroad. Zach was starting kindergarten, and Doug and I had decided to expand our family and had been working on the paperwork for an international adoption. The experience we had in helping bring the baby to her adopted family on the way home from Thailand had a tremendous impact on us, and we decided that we would adopt our second child.

As I had done in the past, I made it public around the company that I was ready for a change and had started discussions about a position for the marketing lead in Australia when our regional director, Bryan, came for a visit to Dubai. He came to meet with me

Photo by Abdalla Altaji

and tell me that he would not approve of me interviewing for the position in Australia. My boss was unpopular with the staff and partners and was becoming a liability to the company. As a result, leadership in Redmond agreed that I should stay in my role as a stabilizing presence.

This was hard to hear. I was happy to know that the work I was doing was noticed and valued by corporate leaders. At the same time, I wanted them to support me and help me advance my career.

Microsoft was a place with endless opportunities that I was encouraged to pursue. I was now learning a real-life lesson that what the business needed trumped everything, regardless of the personal relationships and respect others had for your work. I reassured myself that other opportunities would come up and that staying was a good long-term career decision. Doug and I had worked hard to establish our lives in Dubai, so staying for a while longer was not difficult for the family. I was restless but would have to wait.

A few months later, the regional director that had visited me in Dubai announced he had taken a new position in Asia. There was new leadership at the VP and director levels, with a reorganization in the works. This changed everything and cemented the feeling that I was ready to leave Dubai for a more significant role, even if it meant giving up the expatriate lifestyle. My declaration prompted another visit to Dubai. This time it was Jack, the guy that had recruited me for the job in Dubai three years earlier. We had worked together several times over the years, and while he was always a good laugh, we rarely agreed on the approach to business issues. Once we finished a quick round of small talk, he came right to the point of his visit. He let me know that, as a result of the leadership changes and reorganization, he and I were being considered for the same position on the newly created regional team. Jack was based in Redmond, and therefore had early insight into the proposed team structure and people being talked about to staff the roles. He continued by sharing that he believed that we were equally qualified for the job being discussed for us and that he had come to tell me in person that if I pursued the position that he would do everything he could to discredit me. I was worried because Jack had access to the decision-makers in Redmond and could tap into the discussions easily. This was the reality of corporate networking.

There was no way I was going to let another opportunity slip by. I had done as asked, and let the Australian position go, but wasn't going to do it again. I started working my network, letting people know that I was ready to move forward and about all of the progress made in the business during my time in the role.

The role on the regional team was a step up and would expand my responsibility to include more business development and geography, including Africa and India. Microsoft was making inroads into countries that were hungry for modern technology. I wanted to be at the forefront of that effort. Getting this job would also mean moving back to Redmond, where the team was based. Doug and I discussed it, and he was willing to move back and knew that this could mean a significant career move.

Jack and I both went through the internal interview process. I was not naïve and knew that I was working in a very competitive culture. However, this experience with Jack was the first time I was faced with head-to-head competition for a position or a promotion.

The business environment that exists even today requires an individual to anticipate what is needed to smooth the way for a move forward. In my case, it was to present my accomplishments, along with identifying a replacement for my position. Bragging about my work was outside my comfort zone; however, I understood what was needed in a new job and the business needs to leave my current job successfully. I had to step up and sell myself. While Jack and I had similar experience on paper, I was much better at developing the relationships to get the job done. He had counted on the fact that I would be hesitant to sell my accomplishments effectively.

I became the Regional Marketing Manager for AIME (Africa, India, and the Middle East). Jack took another position in the company and we agreed that the best course of action was to move past our battle. We had several personal friends in common and both knew from past experience with the company that it was likely we would end up working with each other again in the future.

Lessons

1. When you have the opportunity for an experience, take it. I was wholly unprepared and nervous about entering a party where I didn't speak the language or know anyone in the room. It turned out to be one of the most memorable evenings of my life.
2. As we already learned in chapter 3, *never burn bridges.*
3. Know more than just the business. Unexpected execution tactics, like using a woman to announce the change, was a cultural advantage because the partners had no experience dealing with a woman in business.
4. Priority for leaders in the business is not on individual employee development; it is the business in all cases! Even if you have a personal relationship, don't be fooled. I learned to identify and train my replacements so that the team could continue with little disruption.

ten

Out of Africa

THE TIME IN THE MIDDLE East was exciting and informative. I made friends and allies at work and in the community. On many levels, it was hard to leave. Our lives were changing in almost every way.

Then There Were Four

As we were packing to return to Seattle, Doug and I received word that our adoption application had been approved, and our son would be ready to come home in early December. The process had taken about a year and had involved some significant and heart-breaking setbacks. We were in the final stage, which included two visits to Romania. The first was to attend a court proceeding that would legally award custody and clear the way for the Romanian government to issue a passport for our baby to travel. The second was to bring him home.

We received the court date at the end of October. Doug and I arranged for Zach to stay with a friend in Dubai, and we flew to Bucharest via London. The original plan was that we would be met at the airport by a representative from the adoption agency. He would take us to a small town approximately a hundred kilometers from Bucharest, where we would attend the court hearing, and then on to the orphanage to meet Ionut Florian (Jacob). Following the three-week processing period, I would go back to Romania to pick up the baby. Doug and Zach would return to Seattle.

It looked good on paper, but nothing went according to plan. As we landed in London, we learned that Eastern Europe was in the grips of a major snowstorm, and our flight was delayed. When we finally arrived in Bucharest, the representative was not there to meet us. The weather had impacted the trains and taxis, and nothing could get to the airport. We ended up paying an enterprising guy outside the arrival door for a ride in his private car.

By the time he dropped us off across the street from the hotel, our feet were soaking wet from the large hole in the floorboard of the back seat, and the cigarette butt holding the windows up had also dislodged several times during the trip. We checked into the hotel, called the agency in San Francisco, and found that the road between the small town where the adoption hearing took place and Bucharest was closed. The new plan was to take a train to a city close to the orphanage the following day. We had missed the official adoption hearing. Being in the country sufficed, and we still had time to meet our baby before traveling back to Dubai.

Romania was in the early stages of rebuilding after decades of autocratic rule under the Ceausescu regime. The snow compounded the crumbling infrastructure. Bucharest was full of enormous gray and uninspiring communist-era buildings, and the main thorough-fares were riddled with potholes and little evidence of snow removal. Old-model cars and carts pulled by donkeys or horses clogged the roads. The difference from the ultramodern world of Dubai that we were coming from was jarring.

We boarded a late afternoon train and settled into our compart-ment. Within a few minutes, a family entered the car, opened the windows, and began pulling burlap bags filled with cabbage and potatoes into the compartment. The bags went on the seat and the children on top of the bags. Body heat was the only warmth available on the train, and as night fell, it became clear that few lights worked. As the train gathered speed and rattled north, it would frequently jerk to a stop as groups of people jumped off to make their way into the snowy country with their packages and bags.

By the time we reached our stop, it was well past dark, and we were wearing every item of clothing possible from our bag to stay warm. The platform ended a few cars up, and the snow was thigh high on Doug as we exited the train. We were greeted at the station by the agency representative, Dan, who offered us congratulations on a successful court hearing and adoption of the baby we had never met. Dan navi-gated through the snow-covered streets to a small hotel. We shared a celebratory whiskey and made plans to meet our son in the morning before heading back to Bucharest for our evening flight home to Dubai.

We were welcomed into the office of the orphanage by two women. A few minutes later, a third woman entered the room, holding a skinny but seemingly happy baby. He was our son, Jacob Florin Isler. We spent a very short hour with him before handing him back to the women with a promise to return in a few weeks. Leaving this small child that we instantly loved behind was one of the hardest things we had ever done.

I returned three weeks later. This time, when I took Jake into my arms, I was never going to let him go. There was an additional three-day waiting period and a required appointment with the US embassy before I could leave the country with my son. After our experience weeks earlier, I arranged to stay at the Intercontinental Hotel in Bucharest just around the corner from the US embassy for this waiting period. The night after Jake and I arrived at the hotel, the snow came and didn't let up for five days. Bucharest came to a standstill, the shops, businesses, roads, and airport all closed. Jake and I were snowed in!

Having had a baby, I envisioned holding Jake and playing with him as I had done with Zach. Nothing could have prepared me for how scared this tiny little person was. Developmentally, he was several months behind a usual nine-to-twelve-month-old child and was suffering from malnutrition. His skin was translucent gray, and his hair was a muted, dull red. He always kept his tiny hands in front of his face as if to shield himself. However, he kept a close eye on me through those fingers. He barely made a sound and was stiff and uncomfortable being held.

As far as I could tell, Jake had not been mistreated, but he had never been nurtured either. There had not been a response to crying, no one to hold or rock him. We would ease into these normal activities together slowly. He was more relaxed in a crib, so I spent the snowy days sitting on the floor of the hotel room next to his crib, talking to him and occasionally holding his hand or gently stroking his arm and back. Jake watched me intently between his fingers but never reacted.

The maids would come to our room and speak to him in Romanian, and still, there was no response. The only time he cried was when I tried to bathe him. Water terrified him. He shook and screamed with terror, so after the second attempt, I resorted to using a warm washcloth to clean him up. I was increasingly worried that he had a hearing issue.

Doug and I spoke each evening for an update on our children. I shared my worries about Jake's hearing, the weather, and how I was running low on baby supplies. On day seven, there was a break in the weather. I had been in contact with the embassy several times during my stay, and as soon as I was able to get Jake's newly issued passport, I bundled him up and hurried around the corner for the final sign-off on his US visa, then on to the airport.

I held Jake as tightly as I could as the plane climbed steeply away from Bucharest and toward our new life as a family of four. I didn't know what we would do if he had trouble hearing, but I knew our family already loved him, and we would figure it out together.

With no warning, an item dropped to the floor in the galley across from my seat, and Jake's head snapped toward the sound. At that moment, the stress, fears, and happiness of having this new child hit me, and I wept for the remainder of the flight. He could hear, and everything was going to be all right.

A London-Based Team

A few weeks after our return to the United States, my new boss, the Africa, India, and Middle East regional director, Filipe, called a meeting with the team to let us all know that the Regional Team would be moving to London, not Redmond. My container of belongings had arrived from Dubai ten days before, and Doug was up to his ears trying to reestablish our home in Seattle and settle in with our expanded family. I came home and delivered the news that my new job was based in the UK. Doug's response was, "So, Microsoft is going to pay us to live and travel all over the world—why wouldn't we go?" We stopped unpacking and started repacking.

"So, Microsoft is going to pay us to live and travel all over the world—why wouldn't we go?"

Learning from our mistake with moving Zach, we decided a better way to introduce our new life together and bond our new family would be to sail to our new home on the RMS *Queen Elizabeth II*. The cost was the same. All I had to do was to get it approved by my new boss. When I told him that I would rather spend five days traveling to the UK than one ten-hour flight, he shook his head with disbelief but approved, and off we went.

I knew the Middle East area well. However, Africa, India, the Middle East, inclusive of Israel, Greece, and Turkey, were all at different levels of market maturity with varying degrees of technology adoption. In the months leading up to the move to the UK, I had traveled to London several times and staffed most of my team. The team included two Americans already working for Microsoft in London, one Brit, and one person moving from Redmond, leaving only two open heads that I would later fill with a South African and Congolese. My time in Dubai had given me my first taste of how effective and fun a diverse team could be, and I was determined to repeat the experience. Each person brought a different knowledge base, approach, and perspective. This diversity, combined with the expatriate experience that everyone was having, created a productive, effective, and fun group.

The AMIE Regional Team was unique in many ways, not the least of which was the number of women leaders. Three of the six direct reports to the regional director were women. Having this many women on a leadership team was unprecedented for a technology company, and I believe one of the core factors in our success. The team was highly collaborative, used practical problem-solving, had low attrition and high employee satisfaction. We created a stable, inclusive working environment.

Over the next few years, we opened Microsoft offices, implemented anti-piracy campaigns to protect intellectual property, grew, and trained the emerging solutions partner channel. We introduced new versions of Microsoft Windows and Microsoft Office, hosted Bill Gates's first official trip to South Africa, and held partner conferences in Namibia, Istanbul, and London. I experienced an emergency airplane landing in Marrakesh, went horseback riding on the Skeleton Coast, went on safaris in both Zimbabwe and South Africa, spent time in Jerusalem in each district, and paid respects at the Wailing Wall. It was a fantastic time.

Thorndown Lodge

The second assignment as an expatriate was a much easier adjustment for everyone. We knew how to set up our home and how to find the expatriate community. We rented an old farmhouse that was identified as *Thorndown Lodge* rather than a street address. Zach started school at the local village "infant" (primary) school, and Doug found the local pub complete with a kid play area in the back. Doug was now comfortable in the stay-at-home parent role, and with two active boys, he was busy. He was still the only stay-at-home father in this tiny village where everyone knew one another. England is a Western culture absent the restrictions he had encountered the first several months in Dubai. He volunteered at Zach's school and soccer club and quickly became a loved member of the community.

Jake quickly grew into a lively and energetic toddler. He made up for the lost time and, at eighteen months, was into *everything*. Unlike those first tentative days at the hotel in Bucharest, Jake was now an affectionate baby who loved to sit on anyone's lap. He had a knack for dismantling anything and everything and was so busy undecorating the Christmas tree our first year in the UK that we had to gate him out of the living room. His favorite activity was to follow his older brother around, including climbing out of his crib and into bed with Zach most nights.

I was traveling 75 percent of the time, but our home life was settled and happy. We explored Southwest England and made friends quickly. Both Doug and I had matured and gotten more comfortable with our roles, his at home and mine as a professional supporting the family.

Africa and India were experiencing explosive growth and opportunities for Microsoft. Among the most important lessons I learned as a member of the regional team was the Mid-Year Business Review from the reviewer's perspective. Having this view of one of the company's rituals was illuminating.

As a member of a subsidiary leadership team, we stressed for weeks about how to present our business, ask for help from corporate groups, and ultimately how to secure additional investment. Now in the reviewer's seat, I had to work with each of the subsidiaries to balance requests and to ensure that their business goals aligned with the company's business priorities and were aggressive enough to drive their business forward and return the financial results needed.

The process of Mid-Year Review on either side was stressful, rewarding, and fun. Twice a year, my life was consumed with creating or reviewing stories and reporting results about my current businesses. This setting also allowed for some world-class pranks.

At an MYR meeting before my time, in a late-night work session, someone had sat on a photocopier. Now, occasionally, during an official review meeting, that image would show up in a final subsidiary MYR deck. Not all the participants would receive a copy of this exclusive image. The executive review team knew and were most often responsible for the placement. There was a lot at stake in a review meeting, so having this bit of levity was a fantastic way to break the tension and allow time to refocus. It always felt like you were instantly back in the fifth grade, passing notes, and if the executive conducting the review knew about the image, they never let on.

People are the single most crucial determinant for all business success. An individual or team's ability to identify an opportunity and execute an appropriate strategy to take advantage of that opportunity is the critical element for business success and longevity. My role as a Regional Marketing Manager taught me the importance of diversity and cultural relevance. The products that Microsoft was selling were all the same. The primary functions in every office around the globe were similar; however, who you hired, their standing in the market, and their relationships could determine success or failure. Learning to navigate these conditions required me to gain business maturity and use it daily. I had a higher level of visibility and was identified as a top performer and put in the leadership development program for the first time on the AMIE Regional Team.

How Could This Be Happening to Us?

We had been in London for two years, and I was soaking in the recognition and knowledge. Doug and I decided we wanted another child. I got pregnant quickly. We were thrilled. I scheduled a visit to the doctor to have a fecal thickness test at the end of my first trimester. The test was not a standard practice in the States, and it was the first time I had heard of it. The test took place a few weeks later than ideal because I was traveling. Doug went with me to the appointment, and we got the result immediately. The doctor was concerned.

The test results had come back outside of the normal range and indicated that there might be some problems with the baby's development. I was flying to Seattle the following day for a meeting and could see my doctor there for confirmation.

My OB in Seattle looked at the results, had the same concerns, and recommended more extensive tests. Doug and the boys arrived in Seattle a few days later. At Swedish Hospital, we learned that our baby boy had several life-altering development issues. The hard truth was that if I managed to carry the baby to full term, the chances of survival beyond a few hours were slim, and regardless of the outcome, this had already had a profound effect on our lives. We were devastated. Our first child was healthy in every way. We had gambled on a baby and won with Jake. How could this be happening to us, and what would we do?

I spent hours crying and thinking through all of the things that I could have done to cause this. Had I traveled too much? Had I put my baby in danger by going to underdeveloped countries? Had I eaten the wrong thing? Like many women, I never imagined I would be in this place, having to make this choice, and I couldn't shake the feeling that somehow it must be all my fault.

Doug and I had a happy marriage, wanted this baby, and could afford to raise another child. We also needed to be honest about what having a disabled child would mean to our lives. We talked about the pressure this would be on all of us and questioned if we would be able to handle having this child or not having this child. Neither seemed like good options.

After a great deal of agonizing discussion, we decided to terminate the pregnancy. Our consideration had everything to do with our two other children. They were young and happy. If we could spare them heartache and sadness, that was our first responsibility. Microsoft had graciously provided us temporary housing, so we stayed in the States for three weeks before heading back to London. I think about this child often and wonder what he would have been like. However, I am thankful every day that I had the opportunity to make a decision that was right for my family and me. I made the right decision.

> After a great deal of agonizing discussion, we decided to terminate the pregnancy.

I was anxious to get back to work and focus on things I felt I could control. For the next several months, I was so incredibly sad. I couldn't understand how this could have happened. My career and family were both going along so well. I was utterly broken and devastated. I felt an overwhelming loss. Not that we had made the wrong decision but that we had to make this decision at all. I decided the only way I was going to recover was to go home.

A few weeks later, my first hire on the Sale Support team in Redmond, Trish, and colleague David, came to London for a meeting. She sent me an email and asked if Doug and I would have dinner with them. I had seen Trish a few times over the years while working overseas and always liked her. At dinner, Trish confessed that one of the reasons they wanted to see me was to recruit me to lead their team in Redmond. Their manager was moving back to Australia in a few months, and the team wanted a say in who the new leader would be. I was flattered and thought this was the perfect way for us to move home.

I interviewed and landed the position as the international marketing director for Microsoft Press. Press was the publishing division of

Microsoft, responsible for manuals, educational curriculum on all Microsoft products, and the emerging e-learning business.

We arrived home and bought a house close to Microsoft in February.

Lessons

1. Conventional wisdom would be to choose the more stable route, finding a new job that was Redmond-based and lay down roots for the family. I saw such an opportunity for all of us to experience new cultures that I was willing to risk it. Home is where the family is, not a location on a map or a building.

2. A career move is also a life choice. Success can be defined in several ways and does not always fall within the traditional definition of movement up the corporate ladder. Success can come in the form of a happy and fulfilling lifestyle. I made career choices based on my interest and the adventure a choice offered, not how likely the position was to get me promoted.

3. Working with women is fantastic. In technology, we rarely have the opportunity to be 50 percent of the team. To increase the number of women in the industry will take a focused and measured effort. The business results will reveal that the effort was worth it.

4. Building a relationship and having shared experiences can enhance your effectiveness in business.

5. Making the right decision is often painful and hard.

eleven

Career and Life Left Turn

COMING HOME WAS COMFORTABLE. WE had friends and an existing social network that allowed us to slide back into our lives. We bought a brand-new house that had everything we missed while we were away.

Work also seemed natural. I started my new role with Microsoft Press with my usual enthusiasm and drive. Press was not a core business unit for the company. The sole reason the division existed was to support the software business. I had been with Microsoft for long enough to understand the corporate culture and how to get things done, but Press turned out to be a different thing altogether.

They were not technology people. The software was still a relatively new industry finding its way through distribution channel development, defining relationships, and new business models. The book distribution business was established and had no intention of changing.

My job was to work with publishers around the world to translate and publish the titles from the US list. There was a small number of business development managers that sat within subsidiaries dedicated to MS Press who were tasked with the execution of Press marketing programs, business development, and partner management.

My direct reports were from four different countries and all female except one, David. I was the only female member of the International Leadership Team (ILT), and my manager reported to the publisher. The leadership team was a challenge I hadn't planned for. I was no stranger to being the only female in the room, but this was different. These men had come from the old-school, established, slow-moving publishing business.

Publishing structure, process, and business practices were archaic everywhere around the world, and no one seemed thrilled to have a relatively young woman with lots of new ideas in the room. The resistance to include me or value my contribution in the developing world was based on businessmen's lack of experience working with women. My presence and authority was unique and new, so it made them uncomfortable. This was altogether different. This group of all men working and living in the United States were very used to doing things a certain way and made it clear quickly that they were not interested in changing or having a woman suggest new approaches.

Working in MS Press gave me my first unforgettable exposure to China. The publishing business was big in Asia. Bill G. had made a historic visit to the Microsoft office in Beijing to talk with the government about intellectual property. The company was excited and optimistic about the business opportunity in this vast country that was working to modernize.

Patrick was responsible for business development in Asia for Press and had joined the ILT a few months before me. Patrick had worked for Press in the Microsoft Beijing office and had good relationships with the local channel partners and publishers. He was determined to have me join him for a trip to meet partners and learn about the area as soon as possible. I was enthusiastic, and I hadn't spent any time in Asia since my brief trip to Japan with Doug and our time in Thailand just after we were married.

Beijing in 1998 was just like you see in old movies. The sky was hazy, full of gray soot, and there were more bicycles than cars. I had been to Microsoft offices in many countries, but this one was different. It was wall-to-wall people at desks, seemingly on top of one another. It was a hive of activity. Our agenda for the visit included several partner meetings with both retailers and publishers. Each of them showed me books, movies, tapes, and content of all types being produced locally—most without a license and all in high demand. You could purchase the latest children's books and movies in Chinese almost on the same release date as they arrived in the US market. There was no question that China had the skills and talent to produce materials quickly and at high volumes.

There was no cultural reference for protecting intellectual property. MS Press content and Microsoft software were tangible items that could be purchased. There was no understanding of why, after you paid for something, you didn't have the right to do what you wanted with the product. At the practical level, there was no reference point as to why a product shouldn't be replicated. I had run into this in many countries throughout the developing world, but China was different. The Chinese pirates were more sophisticated, and products looked identical to the originals. The "pirate" marketplace was very well run and had a modern distribution and support model.

China was fascinating, but Microsoft Press was a support division, and being on the second string was never easy for me. I had taken this job with my eyes open, knowing full well that it was not part of the core Microsoft business. At the time, I thought the way to pull myself together after losing the baby was an "easy" job. I wanted to be arm's length from the heat and pressure of the core and answering directly to senior executives. I wanted a break from the hot seat.

I distracted myself with my job, new house, and getting Doug and the boys adjusted. I was doing my best to learn the publishing business and bring some of the energy and passion I had for software into this new discipline.

Things Will Be Easier at Home

Zach had gone to the local village school in the UK. When we returned to the United States, he was six, the age when kids are traditionally in the first grade. In the United States, he would start classes midway through the school year, so I visited the school and showed them some of the schoolwork he had done in the UK. They were impressed with his achievement and were concerned that he was so far ahead that he would be bored in a first-grade class. They recommended that he begin school as a second-grader. He was our oldest child, and we thought this advancement would be a tremendous advantage, so we agreed.

Our first indication that this was not the right decision was his excitement a few weeks into school when he greeted me enthusiastically at the front door and started telling me that he had milk for lunch. I was confused and started to ask what the big deal was when I saw Doug waving his arms wildly behind Zach, indicating that I should be happy and not ask too many questions. It turned out that my academically advanced child had never seen milk in a carton and didn't have a clue how to open one. Being much younger than anyone in his class, he was not about to ask how to open it, so he watched the others until he felt confident enough to give it a try. Milk in the UK and most of Europe comes in glass bottles.

As time went on, we learned with dismay that the milk cartons represented only one of the issues that would impact him. He knew different schoolyard games, and a different vocabulary to name simple items like erasers ("rubbers" in the UK) and sweatshirts ("jumpers"). Academics were only a small piece of success in school for young children.

The challenges settling Jake in America began in the immigration line at the airport. Doug landed in Washington, DC, Dulles Airport with the boys. Doug's parents had moved to Virginia, so we planned on going for a visit before heading back to Seattle together. My practice was to arrive ahead of the family and have a few weeks to focus on work and make sure we had temporary housing, so when they arrived, there was a place to land.

Jake attended nursery a few mornings a week in the UK and was benefiting from the social interaction. Doug found him a spot at the Learning Garden Daycare and Nursery School soon after we arrived in Seattle. He loved it and had the good fortune to land in a class with a marvelous teacher. Best of all, there was a set of twin girls adopted from Romania in his class. We had an immediate community.

For years we had talked about building our dream house in the mountains once we returned to the United States. On a trip to

Seattle from Dubai, we had bought a piece of property in the small mountain town of Leavenworth, ninety-five miles northeast of Seattle. In the 1960s, the town remade itself as a Bavarian village, and a thriving tourist destination was born. The buildings all have Bavarian facades complete with hanging baskets full of petunias in the summer. There is a Christmas-tree lighting festival in December, beer gardens, and lederhosen all year round. The most striking thing about the town is that the surrounding mountains look very much like the Alps in southern Germany. Our property was situated just over two miles up a dirt road above the town and offered a fantastic view of the North Cascades. To build on the property, we would need to excavate, create a road, and pull power to a house site from the main (dirt) road. Building the house became Doug's project.

For me, home and family were a comforting distraction. I was struggling to find my rhythm at work. I had always been successful at Microsoft. I fit well within the culture and understood how to work the system, but MS Press was different. Working in a sideline business, I had a hard time finding cadence with my teams, peers, and customers. I always felt one step off.

My solution to getting back on track after losing the baby was to come home to Seattle. Once I arrived, I was sad, distracted, and still not myself. I felt like an imposter inside my own body. How could this have happened? What did I do wrong? What should I have done differently? I had a life that I could never have imagined. I had a husband who I loved, enjoyed being with, and, best of all, we still laughed together. Two beautiful children, a great job, a new house, and the list went on. But I couldn't get a grip. I was grieving, restless, and uncomfortable.

The only thing to do was to make a massive change in my life. I decided to quit my job! I had been in the right place at the right time up until this point professionally. I never imagined that I would be successful and have the option to quit my job. We had been smart with our finances. If we made some adjustments, we could finish building the house and live more conservatively in the mountains. I wouldn't need to work for a while. Problem solved. Not working would give me more time with Doug and the boys, and I was sure that I had found the answer to making myself feel healthy and happy again.

It was less than a year after I joined MS Press when I told my boss that I was leaving Microsoft. I got dozens of emails, one of which was from the head of HR for the company asking for a meeting. Another was from the VP of international sales and marketing, wanting to know what in the world had gotten into me. I had much the same discussion with both men. Each wanted to know what had happened to precipitate this decision and if anything would change my mind. I didn't handle either conversation well. There were so many issues with the Press leadership, coupled with my unrest, that I couldn't think straight.

Both executives graciously offered to investigate other opportunities for me. I was a rising star with experience and talent that was unique—and a female. I couldn't do it. I couldn't imagine taking another job that would require the energy to have to get to know the people and learning a new business. Working at corporate headquarters needed a different type of energy than in subsidiary offices that were several arm lengths away from the customers using our products. I would drive into the parking lot at a corporate building and see evidence of the incredible wealth that Microsoft had created, displayed in outrageously expensive cars, or go to colleagues' homes that were extraordinary by any measure. I certainly benefited, but this environment didn't feel like me. I had the overwhelming need to run away.

After nine years and four international moves, I packed a small box of belongings from my office and walked out the door of the MS Press building for the last time. Doug, the boys, and I headed to visit our friends Jane and Tim from Dubai. They had a summer cottage north of Toronto, and it seemed like the best place to escape and relax as we started our new life as nonworking people. It was a fantastic week, lots of sun and happy children swimming all day in the lake, roasting marshmallows around a campfire, and dropping off to sleep as soon as the sun went down.

I Just Need Some Rest

We returned to Seattle and headed for Leavenworth to spend the last few days of summer before Zach started back to school. Just after returning to the States, the small piece of property bordering ours—with a tiny log cabin—came on the market. It was the perfect location to oversee the construction of the house.

The events of the last several weeks had been fun, scary, and emotional. I had managed to keep the impact of these significant life decisions at bay and enjoy our vacation but now felt exhausted. Doug and I chalked it up to the emotional stress for the past several months and figured all I needed was some rest. We went out to breakfast, and I ordered biscuits and gravy. Not a remarkable order, if you like biscuits and gravy. I did not. Breakfast arrived, I took one bite, and barely made it to the bathroom. I returned to the table; Doug and I just looked at each other. We both knew I was pregnant!

I was excited and terrified. I couldn't go through another experience like the one we had last time, but we desperately wanted another child. We talked about adopting more and had even taken the first few steps into the process to get more information about a set of twins available for adoption from Russia. Once my pregnancy was confirmed, Doug made it very clear that there was no way in the world that we were raising five children, so we closed the adoption inquiry.

Construction on our mountain house would start in the spring, as soon as the snow melted and the property was accessible. We spent weekends and holidays in the cabin hiking and playing in the snow. We were looking forward to the new baby and living on the mountain full-time.

I had been a runner for many years. A thirty- or forty-five-minute run early in the morning kept me sane and held jet lag at bay while I was working all around the world. Since being pregnant, I had started walking Zach to the bus stop then continuing for a few miles. It was at the bus stop that I met one of my closest friends, Kristi Hayne. Kristi's daughter and Zach were both in third grade. Kristi had two daughters—her oldest daughter was a biological child, and her younger daughter was adopted. We immediately had common ground and lots to talk about during our morning walks.

By late winter, there were some minor complications with my pregnancy, and bed rest was ordered. Each day, Doug would pack a cooler with snacks and leave it by my bed in the morning and go about his day. The boys would visit before school, do homework and read with me after school and before bed, and friends came and went. I read until my eyes were blurry. I had three doctor appointments each week. Monday and Friday were nonstress tests, and Wednesday was an ultrasound day. I was bored out of my mind but determined to stay healthy and keep the baby healthy.

Doug drove me to the doctor on Good Friday. The medical assistant placed an instrument on my belly to listen to the baby's heartbeat. She moved the device around a few times and turned to me and asked, "The baby was fine on Wednesday during your ultrasound, right?" I dissolved in a weeping mess. I couldn't bear it if there were anything wrong with this baby. The young woman rushed out of the room and returned with the doctor.

He took my hand, immediately placed the instrument back on my belly, and we heard the even rhythm of a strong heartbeat. He used a portable ultrasound to ensure all was well, then turned to Doug and me with a proposal. It was Passover and Sunday was Easter. He proposed that we all go home, enjoy the holidays, and meet on Monday morning to have a baby. The baby wasn't growing at the rate he would have liked, and my stress wasn't helping things. We agreed, and Lucas Carney Isler arrived Monday afternoon, April 5, 1999. Lucas was tiny, barely six pounds, and after his first few tense minutes in the world, he seemed to be healthy. I celebrated with a can of Guinness beer and a pulled pork sandwich in my hospital room!

The boys loved their new brother, and we settled into a family of five. Construction was underway on the house, and we were busy raising our family.

In for the Long Run

I resumed our morning walking ritual a few weeks after Luke was born. I was itching to start running again. One of the other mothers at the bus stop had a child with diabetes and told Kristi and me in passing that she was going to run a marathon to raise money for juvenile diabetes. The race was in Hawaii the following June. Kristi and I decided to join her. Running would be a fantastic way to get back into shape, and we had a year to get ready.

We started training, raising money, and planning our trip to the big island of Hawaii in June 2000. I had never been a great athlete and am not the most coordinated person. I could never get the hang of aerobics class; I cannot follow the instructor making graceful dance moves. Running was a repetitive action, one foot in front of the other, something I could master. Throughout the year, I ran all the local events, including Sea Fair, Jingle Bells Run, and the St. Patrick's Day Dash. I even ran a half marathon in Olympia,

Washington, and proudly brought home the second-place medal for my age group. Never mind that there were only two people in my age group, and I was the last runner to finish the race. I took home the silver medal and bragging rights.

The significance of running and completing this marathon became about achieving a goal. I had left a successful career to spend more time being a wife and mother. I felt that, somehow, my focus on work had contributed in some way to losing our baby. Having a healthy baby, building my dream house, and living close to my friends represented a second chance to get it right. What I hadn't counted on was that things don't always go as planned.

Lucas was a small baby and was often ill. He didn't eat or sleep well, which meant I was sleep-deprived and frustrated. I had no control over my life and felt that the one thing women are supposed to be good at was being a mother. I loved my children and spent time making meals and baby food from scratch, decorating their rooms, doing crafts, and trying to help in their classrooms. But the reality was, I wasn't any good at it. I didn't have anything in common with the other mothers: I didn't have a great eye for home décor, and I was terrible with a glue gun. Training for the marathon was in my control and represented my release.

I put my screaming baby in the jogging stroller, and off we would go, both sobbing. Luke and I covered hundreds of miles that first year of his life in the name of training and sanity. Crossing the finish line in Hawaii was a personal victory. I accomplished what I set out to do, and I felt triumphant and back in control. I was getting the cadence back in my life and the confidence that I could regain my self-worth.

By most accounts, I am an extrovert. I love socializing, planning events, and being with people—until I don't. I have always relished the time alone on a long-haul flight or in a hotel room or restaurant by myself. I have always needed time to recharge, reflect, to be anonymous. Since leaving Microsoft, I had not had that opportunity. I jumped into family, was pregnant, then had an infant who needed my attention. I spent an additional day in Hawaii following the marathon. Sitting by myself looking over the ocean, relishing the accomplishment filled my soul. I flew home, ready to take on the next chapter of my life.

Lessons

1. When you are stressed or are having to deal with a difficult situation, deviating from normal behavior is rarely the answer. Taking the "easy" job ended up being much harder on me. I had the added pressure of frustration and feeling out of place. It is impossible to bring your authentic and best self to a situation where you feel out of place. Be honest with yourself about the consequences of your decision and the impact they will have.

2. Take a long, deep breath before making big life decisions, especially when they are emotionally based. Remember to leave the door open to walk back through if you find you have gone too far.

twelve

Back to the Basics

OVER THE NEXT YEAR, MUCH of our focus was on building the house. Building season was short, April to October, and that spring would be the third and final season of building.

We moved to the mountains during spring break. Our thinking was that having the boys finish the school year in Leavenworth would allow them to meet kids to play with during the summer. Our house sold on the first day. We could now start our life in the mountains and oversee the final phase of house construction.

The "cabin" we purchased was eight hundred square feet with one bedroom, one bathroom, an antique stove in the kitchen, and a loft. We outfitted the tiny bedroom with bunk beds and a crib and adopted a cat to control the mice. We also put a queen-sized bed in the loft and took advantage of the warmer weather in eastern Washington by incorporating the large covered front porch into the living space. We hung boat netting to keep Luke from tumbling off the porch, installed a tetherball pole, and had a huge truck full of sand delivered in the yard for the boys to play in. Zach started fifth grade and Jake kindergarten in Leavenworth the Monday after Easter. I was training for a second marathon, so Doug would drop the boys off at school in the morning, and I would head up the dirt road with the dog. Life seemed simple, and just as we had hoped those first few weeks.

By the time school was out for the summer, we had met a few families and were trying our best to settle in. The public pool was a lifesaver! It opened the first day of summer break, and I signed Jake up for swimming lessons, Zach up for swim team. Things were looking up.

We moved into the new house the weekend before Thanksgiving, just days before the first snow. To mark the occasion, we hosted a move-in and unpacking weekend for several of our Seattle friends. The house was amazing, warm, and comfortable for our family with plenty of room for friends. The house was the foundation we had dreamed of building for our family. The holiday season was magic.

That first spring and summer living in the mountains, I canned every fruit and vegetable in sight. I made jams, pickles, sauces, and bread. By September, I was bored to death! I had worked my way onto the city's Economic Development Committee and made friends with the Port Commissioner in the next town over and started consulting on projects to develop business in both communities. I still needed something more to occupy my brain. I didn't have a lot in common with other mothers, and was terrible at crafts. I was twenty-five years younger than my peers on the committee and wanted to move faster and more aggressively with economic development initiatives. I needed more to do.

Predictable Engagement

Our second autumn in Leavenworth, after the boys had gone back to school, I went to visit my uncle, who had been ill in Mississippi. On the flight home, I ran into a friend of a friend and learned that she had just sold her travel technology business to a global leader in the space and was struggling with the integration. After a few minutes of chatting, she asked what I was up to and if I would be interested in coming to talk with her about a consulting role. I jumped at the chance.

A few weeks later, I started consulting at Hotwire, a travel platform that had been acquired by Cendent Inc. Hotwire had just over a hundred employees, and Cendent Inc. wanted to integrate some aspects but leave some functions independent. The Hotwire team were entrepreneurs; they were innovative and responded to customer requests for new features or adjustments quickly. This approach worked well when they were a small independent business. However, growth had come quickly, and there had been no time to create a process to incorporate customer feedback or agree on feature prioritization strategy. My job was to develop process and order across essential independent functions.

I relished the challenge of endless meetings and impossible deadlines. I was back on my feet. Right or wrong, my self-worth is very connected to my career, and having a professional identity again made me happy. I rented a small apartment in downtown Seattle and spent two to three nights a week there. I attended economic development committee meetings once a month in Leavenworth and spent quality time with Doug and the kids on weekends. For me, being the best parent is about being the best me and feeling happy. Work and feeling successful makes me happy and a better parent.

At home, the houses and property were significant and required constant work. In the winter, access was via snowmobile, which added a level of complexity and time to every trip into town. The job of maintaining a property with two houses meant there was always something to keep Doug busy. Jake and Zach were in school, so we agreed that Lucas should attend preschool a few days a week. Since moving to Leavenworth, he went to a local in-home day care when we needed a daytime babysitter. He liked being with the other kids, and with my schedule in Seattle, Doug could use the time around the house and for other activities with the older boys.

We had befriended a family whose three kids were close in age to ours. The two older children went to school with Zach, and Jake and their youngest (also named Luke) were attending preschool at a local church. The wife, Alex, offered to start a carpool with Doug and take our Luke to preschool then to her house for the afternoon when the snow came. This arrangement would reduce the number of trips Doug needed to take down the mountain on a snowmobile. It sounded perfect.

I threw myself headfirst into my work. I wrote job descriptions, reorganized teams into specific disciplines with a defined scope of responsibilities, handoff points, deliverables. I worked with the CTO to formalize development and customer input processes. I was spending four nights a week in Seattle. Occasionally, Doug and the boys would make the trip west across the mountains and spend the weekend in the city with me as a treat.

My weekends in the mountains at home were wonderful. As I drove across the mountain pass Thursday afternoons and approached

Mountain Home Road, I began to relax and plan a weekend full of playing with the boys, hiking, and cooking.

In early summer, the kids started talking a lot about the time they were spending with Alex and her children. I didn't think much of it as she was helping us out with carpool and letting Luke spend a few afternoons a week with her and her son between the time preschool let out and Doug picked the older boys up after school. I heard how Alex gave them ice cream, about times when they all went to the river or the playground after school. It all seemed innocent and reasonable. I would always be there on Friday afternoon for school pickup. Lucas and I would spend Friday playing Power Rangers or hiking before picking up the older boys.

There was a charity function in town on a Thursday evening, and I was coming from Seattle and met Doug there. We were seated at a table with Alex, her husband, and two other couples. During the evening, Alex and I were in the ladies' room when I mentioned that I would rather she not give the boys so many sweets. Luke was still tiny for his age and didn't eat well in the first place, and Jake would live off of sugar if it were allowed.

Her response completely shook my world. She told me that she felt she needed to love and care for my children since I wasn't doing it and was away so often. I couldn't see or breathe. Her words felt like a kick in the stomach. It took all my energy to regain my composure, but we were in a public place in a small town with everyone we knew within earshot of the ladies' room. As calmly as I could, I asked her to back away from my children and assured her that I was fully capable of caring for them without her help or input.

I returned to the table and told Doug that we had to leave immediately. He was understandably confused but agreed. At the car, I recounted the conversation and burst into tears. He was silent. I had expected him to agree with my outrage and comfort me. He didn't make a sound. He didn't reassure me that she was out of line, or tell me that I was a good mother. He didn't agree that some distance would do everyone some good and they had all become too dependent on her. I felt as though the ground had fallen out from under me. As we walked into the house, he told me that Alex was an essential part of their lives. He reminded me that it was a small town, and if I made a fuss, everyone would know. And he went upstairs to bed.

I stood in the entryway of my dream house, with my three beautiful children tucked into bed, with the overwhelming feeling that my husband had just walked away from our marriage. Why hadn't he hugged me and said it would be okay? Why had he defended another woman's approach to raising our children? Was I going to be forced to decide between staying in Leavenworth as a full-time mother and having a career?

The pain and silence between Doug and me continued to grow through the rest of the summer. I would arrive home on Thursday afternoon to hear all about swimming in the river with Alex and Dad, or about when they went for pizza and ice cream with Alex and Dad. It was crushing. Doug would not talk about it. There were always six children with them, so I was reasonably sure that the relationship wasn't physical; however, it was increasingly clear that there was an emotional entanglement filling the space that my Seattle life had created.

On my fortieth birthday, I had been working in Seattle for a year. I had a studio apartment on the top floor of the Harbor Steps that we called the "Chick Pad," where I spent at least four nights a week. My favorite aunt came from Mississippi to celebrate and see the boys. I picked her up from the airport and headed for Leavenworth late that morning. We picked Lucas up and went to lunch before picking the boys up from school.

I had made a point of asking Alex directly to stay away from my children and husband again a few weeks earlier, and Doug had agreed that he would manage without the carpool. As school let out, my mobile phone rang, and Alex's name came up as the caller ID. It was Zach telling me that Alex had picked him and Jake up from school and that they were going to her house to play. I pulled into the school parking lot during the conversation and parked directly next to Alex's minivan. All five kids looked up, surprised to see me. I was hurt, outraged, and angry.

I looked her straight in the eye and asked if I had been unclear when I told her to stay away from my family. The children were silent. Zach quickly grabbed his and Jake's backpacks, and they got out of the van and into my car. We had never talked with the children about the trouble Doug and I were having; instead, we explained that the carpool arrangements had changed. They could feel the tension at home, but we did our best to keep things together around them.

The idyllic image of raising my family in a small, close-knit town had been an unrealistic vision. I was naïve to think that I would be able to carve out a life so different from what I had experienced to date. The mountain setting was beautiful; however, what I found was a community with a different perspective and vision that I had very little in common with to build relationships. I stood accused of being a bad mother, too career-focused, and now I was losing my marriage. My dream home became a nightmare, and it was time to regroup. I asked Doug to see a marriage counselor. He declined.

I returned to Seattle, found a counselor, and began seeing her once a week by myself.

Lessons

1. Be kind to yourself and take the time you need. Women and mothers are often too busy with others to take time out to recharge. Not taking the time will impact how you show up for those that love and depend on you.
2. Sometimes there is no right answer and no quick solution. Continue to be present and take one step at a time.
3. Fight for your relationship even when you are the only one fighting. I don't give up easily, and taking chances to save my relationship was risky but worth it.

thirteen

Looking for My Community

There Must Be a Mistake

While my home life was a mess, I found it increasingly easy to find comfort and success at work. I realized that as much as I may have wanted to be the world's best mother, staying home and devoting 100 percent of my energy to motherhood and homemaking was not my path. I had to be honest with myself that a professional identity was essential to me. I needed the positive reinforcement I got from work more than ever. I had been working in the city for a year, and my friends at Microsoft were encouraging me to come back to the company.

Microsoft was still growing like crazy. They had recently acquired three companies that positioned them as a critical player in the enterprise space and created many new opportunities. I needed some stability, and I had been successful in this environment and knew I could be again. I interviewed and accepted a role in the Worldwide Partner group.

I had been away from the company for five years: a lot had changed. The first change I encountered was employee levels. I left the company with the title of marketing director. The title was hard-fought because, at the time I was in Microsoft Press, the men on my team were titled as sales directors, but HR had wanted me to be titled a group manager. I fought and won the battle that marketing was of equal importance to the business and that customers needed to see me as an equivalent to sales directors. Titles matter because they are associated with a level number, salary band, and stock award range. I left the company at a senior level. The leveling system had changed, and I was assured by the recruiter and hiring manager that my new level was comparable with what I had when I left. I was required to sign a document agreeing not to discuss my position level of compensation with anyone. Therefore, I had no way to verify the information HR was providing me. I would quickly find out that this was not the case and that my new level was substantially lower.

I attended the new employee orientation for a second time. My first orientation was nine people. This time there were over a hundred new employees starting work at Microsoft that same day.

With the paperwork completed, I got my office location, and I thought there must be a mistake. I was hired in the WW Partner team who were all located in Building 22 on the main campus. My office was in a satellite building over a mile away. When I finally found it, I learned that I was sharing an office with someone from a completely different team. I had a decision to make about how I was going to react and move forward. I could either take a deep breath and figure out how to succeed under less-than-ideal circumstances or wallow. I was disappointed with the reception I had received, but I knew that I could improve my situation. I had no direct reports, and my manager was from Great Plains Software, one of the companies that had been acquired by Microsoft several months before. Rather than spending time in the remote outpost office, I began working from the cafeteria or small collaboration areas in Building 22 with the rest of the partner organization. I spent time meeting new people, reconnecting with others, and taking on projects that would provide visibility.

There was a regional meeting for the partner team planned for February in Amsterdam. I knew many of the team members from my time overseas, so I secured an invitation to attend that meeting. I missed the world and wanted to find a way to move back into an international role. It didn't take long; at the end of the three-day meeting, I had secured an introduction and recommendation for an open marketing role in the Eastern Europe Regional HQ team.

You Will Love Spring in Munich

Things between Doug and me continued to be strained and distant. We spent time on weekends and holidays focused on the boys rather than on our relationship. I continued to see the counselor and use strategies she suggested to communicate my feelings without blame or anger. I loved Doug and wanted to work this out and keep our life and family together.

I visited an attorney to understand all of my options. She was very clear about the situation and told me that if Doug and I divorced, he would get everything: the boys, the house, and income support from me. I had a residence in another city, had a steady income, and would have minimal grounds to disrupt the children's life for shared custody or anything else. Divorce was not what I wanted, but this was a sobering view.

A few weeks after the meeting in Amsterdam, following a phone interview, I was invited to Munich to meet the team. The assignment for the Munich interview was to develop a strategy for integrating the newly acquired products into a Microsoft mid-market offering to partners. I had ten days to prepare and present my plan.

I read everything I could on Eastern Europe and how investment in the new EU countries and structural funding was affecting business. What technology were companies using today, and how could they use the new sources of investment to accelerate the modernization? Russia was the key market in the region, but the Czech Republic, Poland, and Hungary had more sophisticated/Westernized businesses with less piracy. There was so much to learn and so much opportunity.

My interview journey started with an overnight flight to London, continuing to Munich the following afternoon. I boarded the plane in Seattle with a head full of facts and stacks of notes. I employed one of my tried and true working strategies. I love airplane work and do some of my best work with the hum of the engines in a small seat. As soon as we took off, I ordered a glass of wine and launched Power-Point on my laptop. A few hours before landing, I had a slide deck that I felt good about and settled in for a nap.

BAVARIA IN THE spring was magic. I was staying in the city center and went for a long walk in the English Garden and historic

Marienplatz square as soon as I arrived. I immediately felt at home and loved the feel of the city.

The next few days were full of interviews, dinners, and touring neighborhoods. On my final day in Munich, I had lunch with the hiring manager, Niels. He ordered wine for both of us, and I braced for an offer. When it came, there was one sticking point. The listed position was a lower level than was discussed. The explanation was that the international leveling system was not the same as in the United States, and that a field role was comparable to what I was doing at corporate. I had learned my lesson on this one and stood my ground: the job offer needed to be a promotion for me to accept. This type of negotiation has always been hard for me. I loved Munich, and the idea of moving the family to Germany far away from our troubles in small-town Washington was appealing. This team liked and respected me. This was the community I was looking for when I rejoined Microsoft six months earlier, and I knew I would be successful and could regain my balance with this type of move. Niels agreed to uplevel the offer, we toasted, and had a wonderful lunch before I headed to the airport.

I Took a Job in Munich—Are You Coming?

I hadn't been candid with Doug about the reason for my trip to Munich. Since rejoining Microsoft, I had traveled a fair amount, but since I was gone most weeknights, these trips did not impact on him or the boys. This trip was different in many ways. I was arriving back in Seattle on Thursday night and knew that I would be too tired to make the two-hour drive across the mountains, so I suggested that they spend the weekend in the city. We visited the science center and had pizza on Friday. The boys stayed with friends on Saturday night. It gave Doug and me a chance to talk.

I chose a restaurant close to my apartment, and we made polite family business talk over a drink. I was so nervous I could barely think straight. I had accepted the job and agreed to a start date in June. I was about to take the biggest gamble of my life, telling Doug that I had taken a position based in Munich and agreed to relocate in sixty days. I felt sick. If he said no, I would lose everything.

I took a deep breath and explained that my trip to Europe had not been a regular business trip; instead, it was an interview for a job based in Munich. I told him that I thought a fresh start was what our relationship and family needed. I loved our house, but the lifestyle was not what I wanted. I didn't want to live apart from him and the boys, and I didn't want to choose between having a career and having a family. He listened quietly. I finished and waited for what felt like hours for him to respond. He calmly asked me, "What day do *we* move?"

A ten-thousand-pound weight was lifted off of my body. For the first time in a long time, I felt happy and like we had a path to rebuild our marriage. The move was a project that we could focus on together. Sixty days would pass quickly, and there was a lot to do. Moving a family of five with school-age children was much more complicated than moves we had done in the past. We were up for the challenge.

Taking this job was the second time in our marriage I agreed to a significant life change before consulting him. By this time, we understood the roles each of us played in our relationship. My part centered around the big picture and long-term vision. His contribution was to map the steps to reach our destination. Having the clarity of who does what in a partnership is a critical element for success. Understanding one another's strengths is a formula for building a long-term healthy relationship. The decision to move together gave us the ability to talk openly about the problems we were experiencing in our relationship. Over the years, I had asked a lot of Doug: to leave his career, be the primary parent to our three children, and put his life on hold to support my career ambitions. This was not the norm at the time, but a willingness to take risks and follow his heart regardless of what others thought was one of the things I loved most about him. Agreeing to give up the stereotypical husband role and follow me wasn't easy. On some level, I understood his attraction to a woman that pursued him and paid attention to him, and I couldn't fault him for that. I realized that I took our relationship for granted and assumed he would always be there. We had many issues to work out; however, taking this step together was heading in the right direction.

Lessons

1. If you have doubts, verify. Continue to ask questions. Assumptions can have long-term consequences. In my case, it took much longer for me to receive a salary increase because I started in a low salary band, and there were policies on the amounts of increase I could receive.

2. Giving up is not an option! When you know that you are headed in the right direction, and there are detours or obstacles that set you back, look at them as part of the journey and not a reason to abandon the vision. Stamina is an attribute. Build it whenever you can: it will come in handy many times in life.

3. Sometimes the solution is multiple steps away. Plan a path to get where you want to be and count on each step to bring you closer to the goal.

4. Negotiation is hard! Understanding what you are willing to live with and being firm with what you want will win every time. So often, women, including me, will take the way of least resistance. We assume that the offer presented is the final offer. It rarely, if ever, is. Believe in yourself and your worth and *ask*.

5. Trust yourself. You know you and what you are willing to risk achieving a goal. My goal was to save my marriage and family *and* to have an exciting career. I wanted it all, so I had to aim big and trust that the foundation I had laid in my relationship was strong and would prevail.

fourteen

Central European Time

Lessons to Be Learned

I gave notice to my manager and started building a Redmond-based network of people I would need to be successful in Munich. I knew from experience that making contacts at corporate would be invaluable once I was out of sight and became just another email from the field in the corporate team's overflowing inboxes. Connecting with product teams and the individuals leading "field" programs was critical to getting attention and funding. Central and Eastern Europe (CEE) was a small sub-region that reported up through EMEA (Europe Middle East and Africa). I was on a mission to make sure that the right people knew me before leaving

Redmond. CEE had tons of opportunities, and I was determined to capture that business for Microsoft.

The regional team that I had worked on in London was comprised of people who had come from all corners of the world. The Central and Eastern Europe team was composed of talented people who had risen through the ranks of surrounding subsidiary offices. I was part of an expansion of resources that had started about a year before I joined to handle the increased volume and complexity of the business. As with all small startup teams, the talent and skills needed to grow the CEE subsidiaries with the influx of EU funding, warming relations with Russia, and peace in Central Asia were different than those required to open offices in the twenty-eight countries that the CEE region covered. One bonus of my new job was that my friend Dave, from Microsoft Press, was also working in Munich. He was fluent in German, and an instant tour guide and ally.

There was a crucial regional leadership meeting planned for a month after I officially joined the team. I was on the agenda to present a detailed channel development strategy and execution plan for mid-market and licensing partners in the CEE region. Nothing like jumping in the deep end.

I introduced myself to the subsidiary teams and partners and dug into the business processes. Leading a line of business as a member of the regional team is the ultimate in-between position. On one side, you have corporate constituents that create a global strategy. On the other side are the subsidiary teams that are on the ground every day talking with customers and partners, who are evaluated and compensated for executing the global strategy. The trick was to get and keep all their attention. Success is a great balancing act.

As in the past, I arrived in Munich several weeks before the family and submerged myself into my job and exploring the city.

Rough Trip?

The day finally came when Doug and the boys arrived in Munich. I was anxiously standing in the arrival area when Zach came through the door with a huge smile, pushing a trolley with bags piled high. A little way behind him came Jake with a Band-Aid over his left eye, a cut over his right eye, and three long scratches down his cheek. Next, Luke appeared with a large bald spot on the front left side of his head, and finally, Doug bringing up the rear with more bags. My heart jumped at seeing them, but I was also a bit alarmed at the shape they were in. It looked like it had been a rough trip.

The trip itself was anything but rough. The ticket agent in Seattle took one look at the all-male traveling circus and confirmed that Doug was flying to Munich with the boys alone and upgraded them to business class. I am guessing that would have *never* happened with a mother and three children. When I finally had the opportunity to interrupt and inquire about their wounds, I found that there had been an altercation a few days before they left Leavenworth, and blood was spilled. These types of sibling fights were not an uncommon event for our two youngest children. In the eight years since Jake had joined the family, he had thrived. He reached and surpassed all the physical milestones. He was healthy, happy, and tightly bonded to all of us, mentally and physically. The one deficit that remained as a result of his early months of little stimulation in Romania was his maturity and executive function. He was curious and friendly; however, he had a hard time understanding the consequences of his actions. These deficits often put Luke and Jake head to head. When a physical fight broke out, we would have the boys sit together on a chair until they worked the problem out. Nine times out of ten, the forced togetherness ended in giggles within five minutes. We also employed a two-step process for tattling. If one of the boys approached us to tattle on the other, our strategy was to have them stop and say something nice about the other before snitching. It took them so long to think of something nice to say that the tattle would be forgotten.

My somewhat beat-up and excited family was ready to begin our European adventure. It wasn't until that moment when I truly relaxed and believed that Doug and I would move past our troubles and put our relationship back together.

A few weeks later, our container arrived. We began moving into the house I had rented in the village of Lohf, a kilometer from the Microsoft office and a short drive to the Bavarian International School (BIS), where the boys would attend school.

We found an Italian restaurant, Caruso's, that became our anchor in Lohf. It was between my office and our house and became the standard Friday night dinner venue. We never read the menu. Sebastiano, the owner, would greet us at the door and ask what we were in the mood for, and within a few minutes, wine and dinner would arrive at the table.

BIS was indeed an international school with families from every country imaginable. Most, like us, were on temporary job assignments, so there were few issues with being a new kid in class. Zach had completed the eighth grade in Leavenworth; however, this move allowed us to put him back into the grade with his peers. Although he was a good student, we knew he would benefit from the additional time to mature that repeating the eighth grade would allow.

Luke started kindergarten and was predictably unhappy about leaving us to spend the day in a new environment. He earned the nickname "the broach" early in his life, because I wore him like a piece of jewelry that you pin on each day, and it was still fitting. He was happiest in very close proximity to Doug or me and would follow us around the house or play where he would have a view of one or both of us. When we picked him up on his first official day of school, Jake was in his class with him helping to make the transition. For all their fighting, they were close and provided much-needed comfort to one another in stressful situations.

Doug soon became a regular around the school and started substitute teaching. I was again among the very few working mothers in the expatriate community of parents at the school.

Networking paid off again. The time I had spent meeting with the corporate team before leaving for Munich resulted in investment and new pilots awarded to our region. My time on the ground was dedicated to meeting customers and consulting with subsidiary teams on staffing and marketing campaigns. I spoke at internal meetings and countrywide partner meetings. It became clear that Microsoft products were changing business practices and lives in these countries. I was happy, inspired, and productive.

Several amazing women were working in our division. My family affectionately named one of my favorites on the HQ team "Vickie the Greek." Vickie was a powerhouse who didn't take shit from anyone. She took me under her wing from the moment I stepped into the job. When I first arrived, I was given a temporary car by the team admin. I went to the parking lot and discovered it was a tiny car with only four seats and, therefore, four seat belts. I went back to the admin and explained that I needed a larger car because there were five people in my family. The admin looked straight at me and told me in no uncertain terms that I was in Europe now and that everyone was uncomfortable. I was speechless. I was not objecting to the comfort level, just explaining the reality of having a five-person family. Vickie overheard the conversation, walked over, put her arm around me, and said, "Good thing we are not in Greece; you would have to put everyone on a Vespa." I knew I could count on her from that moment. Vickie was straightforward, blunt, and driven. I loved working with her.

The Russian subsidiary leader was a woman named Olga. Olga's connections in Russia made it possible for Microsoft to succeed on many fronts. In Russia, relationships are everything. A woman leader in this type of dominant position was unheard of in the developing world. However, in many respects, Eastern Europe has less of a gender gap than the modern countries in the West. Almost everyone works in Russia, and almost everyone attended school during communism.

Eastern Europe is where I learned about International Women's Day. After hearing a reference to International Women's Day (IWD) several times, I asked a colleague what IWD was all about. She explained that the day was to celebrate women's contributions. I said, "Oh, Mother's Day." She corrected me and told me that women are celebrated for more than being mothers. They are recognized for their social, cultural, and economic contributions in addition to their ability to have children. It was eye-opening. Being a mother is excellent. However, it is not the only part of being a woman that should be renowned. My first few IWDs, I enjoyed the warm, celebratory feeling of the day. Many people brought flowers into the office and wished women well. It wasn't until several years later that I realized the struggle and significance of this day, or what a substantial role the day would play in my life.

> Women are celebrated for more than being mothers.
> They are recognized for their social, cultural, and economic
> contributions in addition to their ability to have children.

I was excited about the opportunities in Eastern Europe. Investment from the EU structural funds was rolling in, multinational corporations were expanding operations, and Russia had so much cash that it was hosting delegations of Western executives to visit and discuss where to start modernizing their infrastructure, both physical and IT. It was a great time to be in the region and part of this momentum.

The Data Can Tell Stories

Microsoft was experiencing incredible growth in Eastern Europe. I knew the rate of growth was not sustainable and was looking to build a longer-term business process using the data available. I went back to the data for each country, and a few anomalies showed up. Among these were significant transactions in Croatia. These transactions seemed out of place: they were for more substantial amounts than average. I questioned my local team and started digging into the details. I received a phone call late one evening from a woman who had worked in the Croatian subsidiary, asking if I could talk confidentially. Over the next several days, I received calls from people in the Croatian office confirming that the information I had found was in error and assuring me it would be corrected.

The regional VP, Jon, invited me to a meeting. Jon had started in the Czech sub and had worked his way up the company ladder. He was well connected, smart, friendly, and knew how to get things done. Jon asked about the transactions I had uncovered in Croatia and how I found them. I explained the process and that I had asked the local team for additional information. I also told him about the calls I received from a former employee providing information on where other similar transactions showed up. He then asked if I would be willing to give a deposition and explain this to an attorney.

After I recounted the story for the deposition, he asked me to keep the meeting confidential and told me that the corporate security team would be in contact. I was shaken; the transactions were payments between a prominent partner and a leader in the Croatian office. The discovery had put me in danger.

The following day, I received a visit from a member of the corporate security team. He explained that the company was taking additional security measures for my family and me. I would no longer be allowed to travel to Croatia. He confirmed contact numbers for Doug and asked for each of the boys' names, photos, birthdays, and school schedules. He requested that Doug and I remind the school that we were the only people authorized to pick the children up.

It was the early 2000s, the United States had been through 9/11, and the Yugoslavian war was fresh in our region. The CEE business region encompassed all six nations from the former Yugoslavia, many veterans, and those who had lived through the ugly ethnic violence that had consumed the area for ten years. I was an outsider who had stumbled onto business practices that could have severe consequences for the company and individuals, including my family.

High Potential

At the end of my first year in Munich, I was invited to join the EMEA executive development program, "EXPO." I was ecstatic. EXPO was a program that provided exposure and opportunity for top performers across the region and world. Over the next two years, I attended specialized training, received coaching, and an executive mentor. Part of this program was an executive shadowing trip with our newly appointed regional VP. The previous leader had moved on to a chairman role to focus his time and attention on the public sector and strengthening relationship in Brussels. The new leader, Vahe, was another longtime Microsoft employee who had started his career in the French subsidiary and had just completed an assignment in Singapore. He joined CEE just before the annual business review.

The annual business review was always a high-stakes game, amplified for a new leader. Vahe was articulate, personable, and driven. As the leader of the region, he was responsible for presenting all the business metrics, accomplishments, areas to improve, and asks from corporate. Being new to the region, he inherited the good, bad, and ugly. His strategy was to present the plan as if he were looking back from three years ahead. In other words, he framed the region's objectives as if he had accomplished them. This enabled him to focus on the future and paint a picture of outstanding performance. He painted a vivid vision of a successful future rather than dwelling on the current situation that he had not had time to impact. It was brilliant.

As a part of the EXPO program, I accompanied Vahe on an executive trip. The trip had a formal agenda and required that I submit a career plan to the executive before traveling. Career planning is not an area that Microsoft does well, even for the designated high performers. I decided to take a page out of Vahe's book and write a career plan as if it were an announcement being made five years in the future. I made up a job title and supported it with a narrative describing a scope of responsibility that encompassed everything I liked to do and did well. Vahe recognized the format immediately and was impressed.

Our trip was for three days and two countries in the Baltics. I had visited Estonia, Latvia, and Lithuania many times at this point, but this was a completely different pace. We started the day with business leaders, had dinner with government officials, did a debrief and preparation for the next day at 11:00 p.m., email, and off to bed by 1:00 a.m. Breakfast meetings and start the day at 7:00 a.m., fly to the second country, and go through the same schedule there. The trip was exhausting and exhilarating all at once.

On our final leg of the journey, we sat together on the flight back to Munich and had the opportunity to talk about my plan. Vahe provided feedback on observations he made about my executive presence over the past few days and asked clarifying questions about my goals and ambitions. I had been in the CEE Region for three years and had been promoted twice during that time. I was a strong performer and well respected; however, there were other factors at play in the larger EMEA Region that would impact my next move up the ladder.

The company was realigning business and resources, something that happened every few years. There had been several leadership changes in CEE during my time, including the departure of my manager. As a result of the EMEA reorganization, there was a senior leader whose wife worked in the German subsidiary that needed a job. There was nowhere else for him to go, so the decision was made that he would get the manager job. I could stay at my current level or pursue a higher-level position somewhere else. I felt the lump on my head from running straight into the glass ceiling.

Beer Gardens and Pretzels

Munich was just what our family needed. The language was a challenge; however, it was a challenge that we all faced together. The school was a supportive and vibrant community of families, all experiencing life in a similar way. Most were expatriates in Munich for a few years before moving on to their next posting. With this as the backdrop, friendships were made quickly, with the school at the center.

The Bavarian International School was progressive and followed a block class system. The system is based on the belief that peak learning takes place at a different time of day for each child. In other words, some kids learn better early in the morning, so if they have math at the end of the day every day, they will never do well, but if sometimes math is in the morning, their performance will improve.

The result of this system was the class schedules moved depending on the day of the week.

At BIS, this schedule was managed by having Red days and Blue days. On Red Days, a student could start the day with math, then physical education, English, and so on. On Blue days, the day would start with English, science, gym, math, etc. For the younger children, on the days that they had gym class, they would wear their gym clothes to school that day, two to three days a week, depending on the schedule. It was complicated but, by all accounts, resulted in a positive learning environment that gave each student the chance to learn at their optimal time.

Doug had the school system down. Each of the boys had a blue backpack and a red backpack. They knew how to manage the schedule and thrived. The breakdown came when Doug went to the States to see his parents. I was not accustomed to the Red/Blue schedule and out of my depth. I picked the boys up on Monday afternoon and was greeted by eye-rolling that bordered between embarrassment and frustration. I had started the week on Blue when it was Red.

Tuesday morning, I made an executive decision: it was now purple week at the Islers! Luke was horrified, PE was his favorite class, and if he didn't wear his gym clothes on the right day, he could not participate in class. My answer was to have him wear his gym clothes every day for the rest of the week. Jake and Zach took both backpacks each day. I thought this was a fantastic solution. Doug heard stories about the Isler purple week for the rest of the year. I have empathy for any working parent trying to step in and fill the enormous shoes of the stay-at-home parent. Credit where credit is due, kid duty is *hard*!

The purple week episode was another clear example of how domestic routines seem to be just beyond my abilities—in contrast to the success and exhilaration I felt working across the many markets and cultures of Eastern Europe. I don't think it is a statement on my competence as a mother; instead, the ability to recognize this is what sets me apart and makes me a better parent.

Each year, the freshman class at BIS rode their bikes from Munich to Wien (Vienna) and took the train back. The ride took a week and was the highlight of the ninth-grade year. Zach was excited and ready to go. The legal drinking age is younger in Europe, and the laws are often lax. It was made very clear to everyone, parents and students, that there was a no-drinking policy on school trips regardless of a student's age.

A few weeks after the trip, Doug received a phone call from a parent who wanted to share a story of a group of boys that had attended a street fair in Wien on the last night of the trip. There had been drinking, and Zach was involved. I had returned from a conference in Egypt and was in bed, suffering from a terrible case of food poisoning when the call came. In the spirit of joint parenting, when Zach returned home, Doug called him upstairs to our room.

Breaking school rules and drinking is something that most, if not all, high school–age kids are guilty of. The impact of Zach drinking at BIS was potentially life-changing for us. Being an expatriate with a resident permit in a foreign country is, in effect, having an invitation to live and work within that country. If Zach was suspended from school for breaking the law, our resident permit could be revoked, and employment terminated. The implications were potentially enormous.

Zach and Doug were now the same size. Standing eye to eye, Zach finally confessed that the story was true. We were both livid and entirely at a loss of what the consequences should be. Then it hit me. I was still running and planning to enter a half marathon in Paris the following autumn but needed a training partner. Zach was the perfect training partner. School was almost out for the summer, and he would be grounded with no access to friends for the rest of his life so training with me three times a week would allow him to get out of the house. We couldn't think of anything worse for a sixteen-year-old than having to spend quality time with his mother at least three hours a week.

The race also provided an unexpected culture lesson in parenting. To participate in a French race, you need to have a medical release. Doug made appointments for Zach and I at the village clinic. I went straight from work and was in the middle of an EKG, naked from the waist up. I'm not sure who was more startled, Zach or me, when they led him into the room where my test was in progress. In Germany, having family visits together is standard practice. Neither of us has ever mentioned it again.

Zach and I completed the Paris half marathon together on a sunny October morning and celebrated with dinner under the Eiffel Tower. The race followed an unforgettable summer of training. We spent the miles getting to know each other. He loaded my iPod with the latest hip-hop music and regaled me with stories of his first attempts at dating and his interest in world affairs and politics. We discussed his aspirations and answered questions about what I do for work. It was a gift and a time that I cherished with my oldest child as he was becoming a man.

It had taken desire, 5,226 miles, and a few years, but my marriage was back on track. As we navigated the challenges and adventure of a new country, a new school, and a new job, we worked together to rebuild our marriage. We learned to laugh, talk, and enjoy each other again.

WITH NO CLEAR path to advancement in the CEE team and my new manager in place, I started to look for my next job. I circulated

my career plan, and it wasn't long before I had a few opportunities to consider.

One was working in an Online Advertising Platform division in the UK. The General Manager, Sharon, was pregnant and preparing to go on maternity leave for twelve months, standard in the UK. She needed a chief of staff/COO who could step in and run the business in her absence. I didn't know a thing about the Online Advertising Platform business. It would involve managing HR, Finance, 240 employees, and a divisional P&L, and was entirely out of my comfort zone. How could I turn it down!

Sharon of all people had a keen understanding of what it was like to be an ambitious, motivated female at Microsoft. There were very few of us, and many were not interested in helping others. Sharon's journey had made her aware of the issues and determined to support others. Chief of staff came with a promotion and exposure to entirely new business and the opportunity to learn essential leadership skills.

I joined the Online Services Group (OSG) in the UK on December 1, 2007, and Doug started making plans to move to London once school let out in early June.

Lessons

1. Personal relationships are everything in a large company. People move into different roles; taking the time to invest in building relationships that are relevant to your current job is critical. But the long-term advantage of investing in getting to know people will return a lifetime of dividends. The same is true with ignoring the relationship element. The adverse effects of being labeled as unknown, aloof, or arrogant can also follow you throughout your career. Take the time!

2. Committing to a specific project with deadlines is a great focusing function in a new role. Having the pressure to present and make an impression at the start of my time on the new team was the ideal way to learn the business and gave me a reason to reach out to all the local

stakeholders to gather information. I approached them
with questions vs. solutions. It was a winning strategy.

3. Parenting is a constant puzzle, and sometimes doing the
unexpected to de-escalate a situation and reframe it at
the moment is what kids need. Separating children to
their corners after breaking up a fight (physical or
otherwise) will only divide them further and allow them to
rewrite the story of how they were wronged. We found
forcing them together was healing. As Michelle Obama
put it, "You can't hate up close."

4. There is always room for women to help other women. In
technology and other industries, there is the incorrect
assumption that women need to make it on their own, and
there are only a few seats at the table. I don't believe that
is true. Women helping women will improve their business.
If you are short a seat at the table, bring another chair.

fifteen

GMT Round Two

THE UK ONLINE AND ADVERTISING team was having an all-hands, holiday celebration in a swanky London hotel. The General Manager, Sharon, took on big business goals, reshaping her organization, starting with hiring new leaders. Sharon proved to be a master at assembling the team. We immediately bonded, respected, and enjoyed one another. The foundation was in place.

The holiday season was not all about celebrations for field organizations within Microsoft. Mid-Year Reviews started in early January, so December was prep time. My new role as chief of staff for the UK Online Services Group (OSG) meant that I owned the MYR deck and presentation for the subsidiary. I'd been through this business review cycle several times and knew the process well, but OSG was a completely new division to me.

The division had different revenue sources, types of customers, and partner channels. Subsidiary businesses were prioritized for the MYR based on how their revenue numbers impacted the overall global division. The most significant and strategically essential countries were invited to conduct their MYR presentation in person at the Redmond offices to maximize corporate participation. This invitation was often a double-edged sword.

On the one hand, it was great for the subsidiary leadership team to have exposure to corporate executives. The downside was that the room would be filled with corporate attendees who might or might not understand your business and often randomized this discussion or distracted from the points you wanted to land. The UK Online Advertising Mid-Year Review took place in Redmond. Kevin Johnson, a member of the Microsoft Corporate Senior Leadership Team, would attend. No pressure here.

While the Mid-Year preparation was all-consuming during my first several weeks, there was an additional, very high-profile issue that I had the pleasure of managing. The UK Advertising office was in central London, just behind Piccadilly Square. The team had outgrown the space and was in the final phases of construction of a new building across the road from Victoria Station.

This new building was the single most expensive real estate that Microsoft owned at that time, and overseeing the project fell into my scope. There was an experienced construction project manager on my team who, in my first meeting with her and Sharon, burst into tears as she explained that work had stopped on the project and wouldn't continue until we paid the outstanding invoice. The funds were available; however, to use them, we needed the MS Controller to approve a transfer of funds from one bucket to the other to make it happen.

The afternoon of my third day on the job, I called the head of Microsoft Finance, gave him a summary of the situation, and asked that an enormous sum of money be moved from one category to another to pay the construction invoice. Sharon sat mute in the room during the conference call, sliding documents across the table with details to support the answers on how we got into this situation. In the end, he agreed, and the project moved forward. Ninety days later, the organization moved to the new facility.

The business review process proved to be a fantastic team-building exercise for this new UK team. We were all accountable for meeting revenue and business targets. Each member of the group had a role to play in being successful. The master business review deck is a prescribed set of slides from corporate. I put a process in place to ensure that our narrative supported our numbers across each business discipline.

It would be the first time that the Advertising group would follow the corporate standard business review process. I was the only member of this team that had experience in the main software business and knew this process. I knew that there was an unspoken evaluation of how effectively the team worked together during the review meeting that would factor into our overall success. This teamwork aspect would be amplified with Kevin attending our review meeting.

At the end of the first week in January, our UK leadership team landed in Seattle to present the following afternoon. To calm nerves and assure the group that we knew more about the UK Online and Advertising Business than the reviewers, I had wrapped our business review development in the campaign theme "Keep Calm and Carry On," and inserted photos of Winston Churchill smoking a giant cigar or an image of the Tower of London (in case things didn't go well) in decks during our working sessions. I catered meetings with Bacon Buddy sandwiches, shortbread cookies, and scones with clotted cream. I was new to the UK, so I leveraged these small gestures to make the point that this was the UK business, and we were all in it together. The group began to look forward to seeing what kitschy UK item I would interject next. This bit of humor helped to manage the stressful process.

I planned to execute the last phase of my Mid-Year UK campaign during the review meeting in Redmond. The team gathered for a final prep meeting ninety minutes before we were to begin our review meeting. I used the time to go through the meeting agenda, list insights that were shared from teams that had gone before us, and finally I gave each member of the team a piece of paper with a Bee Gees song title on it—"How Deep Is Your Love," "Jive Talkin'," "You Should Be Dancing"—you get the idea. I then instructed the team in a widely known, never-talked-about Mid-Year Review game I had played with several groups over the years. The game is a point-based activity with points earned each time the title of the song you were given is mentioned in your presentation.

The game served two essential purposes: First, the team knew the business and the story backward and forward, so focusing on this new piece of information would ensure that they relaxed and let the story flow. Second, these were songs that were identifiable and out of place so that corporate leaders would recognize the game and see that this very new team had come together and was on the same page. Forty-five minutes into the review, as "Night Fever" rolled off the tongue of the sales director for the second time, Kevin Johnson turned to me and smiled. It had worked. I had brought the team together, and we were able to demonstrate our coordination and willingness to work together.

Keep Calm and Carry On

Telling the boys that we were leaving Germany was a daunting task. Our time in Lohf had been healing for our marriage and beautiful for the family. We hiked in the Alps on summer weekends, skied in the winter, and traveled all over Europe and the Middle East, catching up with friends who shared the global life. We had grown accustomed to the rhythm of shops closing on Sunday, Friday nights at the village Italian restaurant, and February school ski trips to celebrate Carnival. It was sad to leave. However, we were all in the right place. It was time to move on to our next adventure.

The cost of living in London was significantly higher than in Munich, but the career move was right. It would be a lateral move, but this position would offer the opportunity to expand my scope into new areas and a new division, so we went ahead. With cost as a factor, I rented a house in the village of Walton on the Thames, close to The American International School of Switzerland (TASIS), about an hour by train southwest of London. Doug and the boys planned to move as soon as the school year was complete.

Doug jumped into the TASIS school community within the first few days. He resumed substitute teaching in the lower school and quickly built a community that included several stay-at-home fathers for the first time. Our closest friend community became known as the Star Family. A star has a center and many points of entry, and like other expatriate communities, friendships develop fast when you share a common family platform and experience. Our Star family consisted of a Swedish family with three children. The oldest girl was in Zach's class, the youngest boy in Luke's class, and the middle daughter was a year older than Jake. Along with an American family from Texas whose son rounded out the trio of best friends and football mates for Luke and a daughter a year older than Jake.

We settled into life in the UK. Luke could be found on the football (soccer) pitch every break and after school, and Zach began to excel academically. Jake made friends with TASIS classmates and joined a local theater club. Doug and I reconnected with friends from our first tour in the UK. Weekends filled with sports games and pub crawls.

I enjoyed the energy and action of working in central London and threw myself into learning a new business. My boss, a woman for the first time in many years, was very supportive and encouraged my involvement in internal and external women's groups. I had been elected to the Women of Microsoft board while in Munich and had started building a network of women working at Microsoft across the world and in London. I spoke at conferences, industry meetings, panels, and mentored as many women as I could manage.

I began to realize that my story in technology as a woman, as a mother, as a leader, was unique. The question I was asked most often when I told the story of my career was, "Did you bring your family?" I thought this was such an odd question. Of course I brought my family. Where else would they be? It became apparent this was not such a strange question to many women. Many of the women I encountered at events or through mentoring didn't think they had the option to take the risks that I had in my personal or professional life.

> The question I was asked most often when I told the story of my career was, "Did you bring your family?"

For the first time, I encountered unforgiving audiences that pushed back on us for our lifestyle, from both parents and teachers at the boys' school. For some, I was an anomaly, but others disapproved of the mother not being the primary parent. I even had one teacher comment to me at a school function that she was so happy that Luke had a mother because he was the only student that she didn't know the mother. It took all my self-control to remind her that she knew Luke's father, since he taught at the school, and I inquired about how many of her students' fathers she knew. Doug and I had always approached our lives in terms of who had the better opportunity. My job offered the prospect to live outside the United States, and with that the luxury to have one stay-at-home parent.

The chief of staff job, like most others in the company, was constantly evolving. As planned, shortly after I took the position, Sharon went on maternity leave for a year. Several months into her leave, she elected not to return. The global online advertising sales leader, Chris, took over her position for a few months, but ultimately decided that the job was not what he wanted. During this same time, the corporate organization's charter expanded to include consumer products like the Windows operating system and Bing search engine.

The division had a series of leaders, names, and acronyms in rapid succession: Consumer Online and Internet (COI) and Consumer and Online (C&O). Reshaping the business was an enormous change on a global level and ushered in new leadership at corporate and in EMEA. As the chief of staff, I stepped into an acting leadership role. In some ways, this was an ideal situation; it provided the opportunity to demonstrate my leadership skills with more exposure to senior executives. However, there were also drawbacks. I stepped up into this position, and led a considerable restructuring and organizational realignment in the UK business but was never promoted or compensated for doing the work of a higher-level position.

During this transition time, leading the UK online business, I was invited to a meeting with other C&O leaders in EMEA and executives from the Windows Business Group in Redmond. Windows was still the bedrock of Microsoft's business, but within minutes of the meeting, it was evident that this team of senior leaders had little understanding of the online or media business.

The company was gearing up to launch a major Windows update. The leaders were in Europe to discuss leveraging the online media inventory to promote the launch. Very reasonable on the surface; however, each of the business units was accountable for specific revenue targets. The assumption on the table was that we would give the Windows team the media inventory for free or at a vastly reduced rate to support the company's flagship product. Giving Windows inventory would directly impact my ability to reach my target. I explained this issue, proposed alternatives, and agreed to follow up on the discussion. The meeting moved on to other agenda items.

Two days later, I received a call from the Windows HR leader, telling me that Brad, the Windows Business Group vice president, wanted me to come to work for the Windows Business Group to lead the Windows 7 launch. I was honored and a little overwhelmed. Microsoft Windows was one of the world's leading brands. I had built a solid reputation, had support in the EMEA leadership team, and I wasn't sure I was ready to give that up. Moving to a corporate business group was the goal of many of the people in field offices; it was not a part of mine.

Leading the launch of Microsoft's next big operating system was an enormous opportunity, and one not quickly passed up, planned or not.

Taking the job in the Windows Business Group had implications at home. Zach was graduating from high school and planned to attend college in the States. But for Jake and Luke, moving back to Seattle would mean a significant adjustment.

Jake would be entering high school, so if we were going to make a move back to the United States, this was a good time to do it. We had kept our dream house in the mountains as an anchor. Doug and the kids spent time there during summer school breaks, and we all traveled back for a few Christmas breaks and always thought of it as home. Being in Seattle would allow Doug more control over the constant maintenance needed on the property and would enable us to spend more time in this beautiful home as a refuge from city life.

I accepted the position as the Windows 7.0 launch lead in November of 2008.

Lessons

1. Jump in and do the job. Taking on the task of fixing a problem that developed before my time was daunting; however, the job came with good and bad aspects. Being willing to solve an issue will build your confidence and credibility in a new position. Don't spend the time to clarify that it wasn't your fault.

2. When you join a new group of any kind, find a way to bring them together that everyone can relate to. Developing and executing a silly UK theme for a critical business review unified the team. It gave us a shared experience and an inside joke and, more importantly, taught us how to work together effectively.

3. Women assume they can't do a job or follow a dream before considering the possibilities. Much of this is cultural and challenging to overcome. When you dig into the *why not*, often, you find more reasons to go for it than to opt out.

4. Everything is negotiable. I was in a position to lead significant changes in the business scope and people alignment, and the global business adjusted to market conditions. This was an opportunity to be compensated for that work. I had my head down and was focused on getting the job done and, in hindsight, wished I would have acted on this opportunity.

sixteen

Windows on the World

ALWAYS FOLLOW YOUR GUT! WHEN you feel like something isn't right, you don't quite fit in, *abort* quickly. I'm not saying you shouldn't try to work things out in an uncomfortable situation or that you should make a permanent decision about a person because you don't initially hit it off. But when you know it isn't right, don't hang around.

Taking the position as the Worldwide Launch lead for Microsoft's next big operating system seemed like a no-brainer. My experience both at corporate and in international offices was the perfect skill set and sensibility for this job. Microsoft was one of the largest brands in the world, and Windows was the flagship product. I again prepared to move the family across the ocean, but this time the move was home. Things would be comfortable at home. We had friends; we understood the culture, and the grocery stores were open 24/7! What could go wrong?

I flew to Redmond, where Brad, Windows VP, extended the job offer to me. During the conversation, he told me he had just hired a woman from Fidelity Investments, Kathleen, to lead consumer marketing for the Windows team and was looking forward to introducing us. My first call with Kathleen was two weeks later from London. On that call, she explained that the Windows Leadership Team had restructured as part of the realigning, and part of that would be to move me to a position they felt I was better suited for. The new role would focus on international marketing reporting to her. The Windows 7 launch lead would be someone else. The team reorganization before my first day was a sign of things to come.

I traveled to Redmond a few weeks later to meet Kathleen and the team in person. It was a new team, a new leader, and everyone was finding their feet. We had less than eight months to develop a marketing strategy, create support materials, train the field teams and partners to launch the product that would turn the tide for Microsoft. Apple was gaining strength in the market, and we were losing the hearts and minds of our traditional customer base. The previous version of Windows, "Vista," had been a disaster, and Windows 7 was the great hope to gain ground back.

I was uneasy. I had accepted the job of "Windows Launch Lead." The "International Consumer Marketing" position was new, with an ambiguous scope. I would be making it up as I went along, but it was quickly evident that the core of the job was limited and had little business impact. My responsibilities were very similar to the type of work I did twenty years earlier in my first position at

Microsoft. In the fifteen years since being in Corporate Communication, I ran sales teams all over the world, set strategy for partner channels, and had responsibility for business P&L in one of the most significant subsidiaries. I was steeped in the core of Microsoft business and licensing models. I was the only member of Kathleen's team that had experience working outside of corporate. My company network was strong across the subsidiaries, and I knew firsthand the issues facing the Windows business group leads in the subsidiary offices. I felt like none of these facts mattered to my new team or manager. I had made the wrong move, with significant implications.

To make matters worse, I was assigned an office that was on a different floor than the rest of the group. Kathleen described her management style as "in-person," which, as far as I could tell, most often meant the nearest person to her was the one who was in favor. I traveled back and forth to the UK for a few months during the transition period but couldn't help but feel completely disconnected from my new team. The time difference was eight hours and a million miles.

As a part of the launch process, the Windows leadership team went on a tour to the top subsidiaries to review their country-specific product launch plans. Kathleen and I started in Sydney, then on to London and Paris, where other senior executives would join us. Europe was a grueling schedule that included a full-day meeting and dinner with the UK team, followed by a 6:00 a.m. departure to Paris via the Eurostar. I sat with Kathleen for the last thirty minutes of the train trip to brief her on who would attend the meeting representing France, EMEA, and other top European countries. She turned the conversation toward the annual performance reviews, then explained in a very matter-of-fact voice that she had little experience with the Microsoft performance process, but she wanted me to know that she had made performance rating and compensation decisions based on what she had seen of the team since she arrived. I was not in town, so she had seen very little of me. As a result, she had given me the lowest rating on the team, and no monetary reward.

I could hardly breathe; my head started to spin. Only a few months before, I had taken a position with the promise of career advancement and visibility. I had moved my family around the world, and left a supportive leadership team in EMEA. I was a top performer for years; however, none of that mattered. With that rating, Kathleen delivered the message that I was considered a low performer and would have little support from the division executives. The implications of this type of performance review rating are enormous and long term. Not only does this rating affect the annual salary and stock award, but it also precludes you from applying for other positions in the company. It is a vote of no confidence. I was devastated.

As we pulled into Gare du Nord station in Paris, I had to move past my impending emotional breakdown and remain composed. There was a full day of meetings and dinner full of people from corporate who didn't feel I was up to doing my job. That day was one of the hardest of my career.

We rented a house in northeast Seattle in our old neighborhood. It was familiar, and some of our longtime friends still lived close. Zach headed to college in Washington, DC, and Luke and Jake registered for the local public school.

The boys say it takes Doug six months to settle in, and the clock starts the day the container arrives. Our belongings arrived on a sweltering August morning.

As in the past, I was surrounded by company infrastructure. Doug was left on his own to establish the family routines, get the boys into school, sports, and clubs. With all the adjustments, I didn't know how to tell him that I would not be getting the salary increase and bonus because I had been assessed as a low performer in the job I just started. It was too late to tell him we had made the wrong choice in moving back to the States.

I was in a grim position professionally with few options. I had been with Microsoft for over fifteen years collectively. I was the sole source of income, one child in college, with two others and a husband who needed stability.

Attitude is everything, and I am not one to shrink from a challenge. I took a deep breath. The best way forward was to show the Windows division that they were wrong about me.

From that point, I started the long trip back to the top. My strength has always been in forming relationships. I knew I had unique value and insight to contribute. All I needed was to show off my skills. I started going to meetings, whether I was invited or not. I began to share ideas to expose my corporate peers to other global insights, and if included, how they would impact and improve our overall marketing strategy. I successfully sold corporate marketing strategies to the field teams and soon became the trusted advisor on both sides of the field vs. corporate relationship. By the next summer's performance review cycle, I had built a team of direct reports, had ownership of a sizable budget, and a secured seat at the table for strategic marketing meetings. My review rating and awards were significantly better.

Over the next few years working in the Windows division, my star began to rise again. I had turned a low-level implementation role into a Global Integrated Marketing Team. My team transformed Microsoft Windows global campaign approach into an industry-leading practice that delivered culturally relevant execution strategies across thirty-five markets. We improved ROI and sales results, managed local media, and creative agencies on three continents with budgets in the hundreds of millions of dollars. I shared my approach at industry events in Europe and Asia. My performance review ranking was at the top once more.

I was traveling over 70 percent of the time, with a considerable amount in China, India, and Brazil. These countries represented a sizable opportunity for Microsoft with a growing economic status in the world, an expanding middle class, and interest in improving education and business modernization. My team and I developed detailed emerging market strategies that were approved at the highest levels of the company. I was challenged, learning, and having fun again. Doing this work brought back the feeling of the early days with Microsoft when I was making a difference in people's lives through technology.

During this time, there were also changes in the Windows division leadership. A woman was at the helm of the Windows business for the first time in the company's history. I still struggled with Kathleen's unpredictable "in-person" style, but Tami provided balance. She rose through the ranks of finance and was a thoughtful and inclusive leader. I had her support and trust as long as I continued to deliver results.

Tami was promoted to chief marketing officer but left Microsoft within a year. With her departure came a reshuffling of company leadership, a return to a predominantly male team leading the company. Tami leaving was also a personal blow. She had been an ally and mentor, and I felt exposed and vulnerable.

I had worked with women at all levels for years, but being in the corporate epicenter was different. In subsidiary offices, there was a feeling of teamwork; everyone in the office, regardless of your functional group alignment or gender, was focused on meeting the country's revenue and marketing goals. In Redmond, the focus was on beating your neighbor out of the next promotion or bonus, and with few women in leadership, it felt like the Hunger Games. The sense that there was only room for a few women in leadership was palpable and weighed heavily on me, and women across the company. I attended a meeting for senior women in marketing where we were told that there were fewer than fifty women in marketing at the director level or above in Redmond, so we needed to support one another. Microsoft had always promoted and thrived on a competitive culture. The idea that women should come together and support each other regardless of the personal cost to your career seemed out of touch and unrealistic.

Having a woman like Tami at the highest level of marketing leadership inspired me and others to continue driving forward to advance up the corporate latter. Without a lighthouse leader, and with the lack of connection I felt with Kathleen, I began to question if I wanted to stay in this fight. This was exacerbated by the announcement that the new chief marketing officer was a man who had risen through product marketing and never worked anyplace other than Microsoft. His nickname was the "smiling assassin." I had a few meetings with him, but he made it clear quickly that he had no interest in investing marketing dollars outside of the primary US market and didn't have the time or respect for any experience that differed from his own in Redmond. My feeling that I could be successful in this situation was diminishing.

I Have to Leave

My travel schedule was difficult on Doug and our relationship. I was consumed with work, with little time to invest in ensuring things were happy at home. Back in the United States, there was no need to rely on the family team we had built to face new situations, explore new countries, learn how to grocery shop, and order in foreign restaurants. We all went our separate ways with the assumption that we were safe in our native land, so we didn't need to stick together as tightly as we had overseas.

Zach was away at school. Jake and Luke were involved in school and sports. When I was home for a rare weekend, Doug would head to the mountain house for repairs or maintenance. We had met new friends through the boys' schools and teams. We socialized with old friends and a few people who worked at Microsoft living in the neighborhood. By all accounts, we were busy, successful, and happy.

In reality, there were gaps. Jake had always been a challenge; as he gained more independence, there were more chances for him to make bad choices. He found trouble at every turn, which put him and Doug at odds often. We learned of Luke's dyslexia in the UK, and now back in the United States, we were able to get support in the public schools, and he was making academic progress. School activities and club sports made it feel as though there was a commitment every night. Doug was managing it all virtually alone. Being a "drive-by parent," I didn't feel as though I could slide back in after several nights at five-star hotels to offer an opinion on how I would be doing things differently. But I did.

It all came to a head when I asked Doug to join me on a business trip to Sydney. There was a big product launch, and many of the spouses were joining for launch events. I thought it would be fun to have him come with me. When I posed the question, he looked at me and shook his head. His reaction made me mad and hurt. I couldn't understand why he didn't want to run off and have a bit of fun, just the two of us. But as I thought about it, how could he? He was managing our lives while I was spending every waking moment and many sleepless nights worrying about the changes happening at work. I had been so preoccupied with my situation at work, I hadn't even stopped to think about the changes that were happening in his life and how he was feeling. I was taking him for granted, and it hit me that we had truly fallen into stereotypical roles. Only my behavior was stereotypically male. Doug and our relationship was my stability. We had worked hard to recover our marriage when we moved to Europe, and I was determined to never be in a position that we were so distant from one another again.

The latest reorganization on my team was starting to take shape. One positive was, for the first time in my career, there were more women at the table than men on Kathleen's leadership team. The downside was that with so few women in technology management roles, having so many women on one team fostered a climate of rivalry for advancement and recognition. I had worked with teams of women before, yet had never experienced this heightened sense of competition in every interaction. With the absence of strong leadership, the environment was toxic and dysfunctional. I didn't have the stomach for it.

Microsoft had just launched Windows 8.1, my third product launch since coming back to the United States, and this one was fraught with market controversy. The massive campaign budget that Windows had enjoyed was slashed under the new central marketing umbrella. In Windows, I earned free rein to lead international campaigns and manage agencies; however, the mission of Central Marketing had a different focus, which was consolidation.

I learned of plans to reduce my scope and split up my group for the first time in a team meeting with all of my peers. There was a new climate of survival. This type of meeting became the norm and served as an unfortunate example of how women could turn on one another when they feel that their opportunities are scarce. These types of encounters, coupled with my growing worries about how little time I was spending with my family, made me realize that the time had come to take a hard look at my life and career. I was no longer having fun or feeling empowered anywhere in my life. I felt depressed and disconnected and desperately unhappy.

I had struggled with Kathleen's management style from the start and now found myself with a team full of women who thrived in the toxic competitive environment she created, with a division leader that had refocused company resources away from my passions. I left Microsoft for the second and final time in the autumn of 2014.

Lessons

1. Follow your gut. Not following your instincts has lasting consequences!

2. Professionalism and composure are critical, no matter what the situation. Reading the room and managing the message that you transmit makes a lasting impression. Focus on what is in front of you that you can affect at the moment when you are faced with an overwhelming situation. Overemotional reactions are rarely beneficial. This will give you time to digest and calibrate a response.

3. Attitude is everything. If you think you can, you will. Even in the worst situations, having a robust, positive resolve will take you far.

4. Don't hang on too long. I loved my job; however, with the changes to the organizational priorities, it was only a matter of time before my role changed. I was afraid of change and didn't act on what I knew would be best if I wanted to stay at the company.

5. Self-awareness and grace are essential elements of successful relationships.

seventeen

The Beginning

I FELT FREE AND EXCITED FOR the first few weeks after leaving Microsoft. I had no meetings scheduled, no calls to take, no one to answer to. Leaving Microsoft this time represented the opportunity to accelerate my career and move to a leadership position that didn't need to follow the promotions guidelines and compensation model that I felt stuck in. My next job was going to be great, and it could be based anywhere in the world. I started talking with other

BeBold Logo Design: Astronauts & Poets

leading technology companies, but they all sounded just like the one I had left. I wanted something different. In many ways, I was at the top of my game. I had developed expertise backed up by a proven track record running global businesses. I was confident that my skills were transferable to other jobs and industries.

I completed an online application and went through the interview processes with a few notable nontech companies, but each time the process stopped at the same point: "What year did you get your degree?" "What is your college degree in?" "Our policy is only to hire college graduates." I never finished college. I married that guy from the photo shop, went to Thailand, started working at Microsoft, had a family, and never got around to finishing the last few credits to graduate. I didn't think it mattered after twenty-five years of a successful career. But it did. In the back of my mind, not having finished college was something that had bothered me, but I thought I was too old to go back to school. After all, what could I learn that would be useful with a degree at this point?

The last few years at Microsoft had depleted my self-esteem. I was hurt and angry and wanted nothing to do with Microsoft or the Alumni Association. The message that I was getting on the open job market—that I was not good enough for any position because I didn't finish college some thirty years ago—was reinforcing my feelings of inadequacy. I was lost and didn't know what to do with myself, and I had no idea who I was without Microsoft.

Transitioning Is Hard for Everyone

When the kids grow up and move out, it is a difficult transition for any parent who has been the primary caregiver. Doug was again entering new territory. He was always the point person for the boys at home, with school and sports. He had filled his days with managing our house and the kids' schedules. Jake had been Doug's most significant project. He was in his final year of high school, becoming more independent. Aside from Luke's sports schedule, Doug had time on his hands.

One of the success factors in our marriage is that we each had a role to play, and now neither of us was sure what those roles were. We were both struggling to redefine our lives.

Doug had left his career in fisheries to care for our family and support me. When we moved to Dubai, he was on a path to a successful career working for one of the largest Japanese trading companies, with a bright future. He gave that up and had been out of the working world too long to slip back in quickly. Staying home together was not financially realistic or useful for our relationship. We each needed a purpose.

He found his direction at the request from a friend to help a young couple embarking on a house remodel with a baby on the way. Doug had always been handy and did much of the work to maintain our mountain house himself. The first job for friends turned into referrals from subcontractors working alongside him. He started working full-time for a local contractor. His life changed. He was happy, engaged, and is well liked by all their clients.

How Hard Can a Startup Be?

After six months of job rejections, some because I was too old, some because I was old and a female, and others because I didn't have a college degree, I felt lonely, isolated, and overwhelmed. I was struggling to find a reason to get out of bed every day. I have always been the one to initiate Friday night happy hours or weekend dinner parties, but I no longer tried. I had no interest or energy to maintain my community, and my community drifted away from me. My friends knew I was struggling but didn't know how to help. I didn't have a strong community of professional women outside of Microsoft to turn to for support. I was lost.

A friend of a friend approached me with a proposition. He had been working on an idea for a startup for a couple of years, had hired a small team, and had funding lined up. The catch was that his investor wouldn't release the money until he had someone to lead the business. He asked me to be the CEO. I met with the team and the investor. The technology was interesting, and this business was tiny compared to the work I had been doing at Microsoft. I thought, "How hard can this be?" I didn't need a college degree for this job. I was the boss.

I thought, "How hard can this be?" I didn't need a college degree for this job. I was the boss.

I learned exactly how hard it could be! For the next three years, I tried to crack the code of a digital healthcare startup. I developed and redeveloped the product vision, fired and hired people, raised more money, and pitched and pitched and pitched. I was asked by potential investors, "How much longer are you planning to work?" Or, "Are you in the game for the long haul?" One of my favorites was a notable angel investor who told me I needed a young, technically savvy man as my chief technology officer before he would invest in my company. It was just too fucking hard!

There was some success. The company participated in two accelerator programs, brought on customers, and launched a technology service that was integrated with one of the large healthcare platforms.

Being a startup CEO gave me a reason to get up and out of the house, gave me access to a new professional network, and restored my confidence. A year into my startup adventure, I decided that it was time to finish college. Completing my education would set an example for the boys, and it was something that I needed to do to feel good about myself.

I contacted Seattle Pacific University to find out what it would take to finish those eight outstanding credits. The first answer was that I would need to start over as a sophomore because my credits had "expired." Who knew college courses have an expiration date? Since returning to Seattle, I had been mentoring Seattle Pacific University students, and had interviewed and hired hundreds of people throughout my career. Never once had I heard of an expiration date to higher education. I tracked down everyone I could think of to lobby my case. After several months of conversations with admissions, university board members, and my newly assigned advisor, I started the first of two general education requirements courses I still needed. I graduated from Seattle Pacific University in March 2018, thirty-two years after starting college.

The Year of Almost

The money was running out at the startup, so I started to interview for marketing and leadership roles with my newly minted degree. I felt empowered and excited when people would point out that there was an error on my CV or LinkedIn because it said I graduated from college in 2018. I took pleasure in assuring them that there was no error, that indeed, I was a new college graduate.

One of my small investors worked for a fast-growing technology company in Southern California that had been looking for a VP of international marketing a year before. I had interesting discussions, but nothing had come of it, since I was busy with school and the startup. She called me again this time about the chief marketing officer role. The leadership team at the company was all male, and the most significant growth in their business was outside the United States. The timing and conditions were ideal. I was out of money in the startup, the company was interested in adding diversity to their leadership, and I had the unique global skills they needed. Luke was in college, and we were in the process of selling our mountain home. We had no obligations or ties to Seattle.

After three months of phone interviews, I was invited to spend two days on their campus. At the end of the formal interview process, the president of the company asked if I could stay on and accompany him to a meeting about a large project that was underway. A week later, my references all checked out, and I had an invitation for an offer call on my calendar. I thought the job was in the bag.

The headhunter started the call on Tuesday morning by telling me that the good news was that I was still the favorite candidate for the position, but there was a new candidate recommended by a board member now being interviewed. They hired the other person within two weeks. I never heard whether the person was a female, but I doubt it.

Two days later, we received news that the financing for the buyer of our mountain house had fallen through one week before closing. We had accepted the offer on the house two months earlier and negotiated to close one week after Zach's wedding, which we were hosting at our mountain house.

All of a sudden, all of my plans for the next stage of life had fallen apart. I was closing down the startup because we were moving to California for an exciting new job. Doug was planning the move out of the mountain house and quitting his job.

It felt like the year of "almost." My startup *almost* took off, I *almost* moved to California for a big job, and we *almost* sold our mountain home.

Bold Future

Launching a startup while going to school took energy and time. But still, something was missing in my life. I missed being a part of the broader working world. To combat the feeling of isolation, I kept in touch with my global network online and social interactions when they visited corporate. One of those colleagues was Nickie Smith. Nickie had moved to Seattle from London with her two sons and stay-at-home husband just before I left Microsoft. She and I started meeting for drinks to discuss life challenges. Nickie was adjusting to a new country, schools, and building a network, all of which I had experienced and could relate to. My side of the discussion revolved around feeling lonely and ill-equipped to lead a startup. During one of those sessions in early January 2016, Nickie asked, "Why doesn't the US celebrate International Women's Day?" It was a great question; I didn't have a good response. After two glasses of wine, we decided to host an IWD celebration. There were six weeks until March 8, the official date of IWD. We were both energized by the idea.

> During one of those sessions in early January 2016,
> Nickie asked, "Why doesn't the US celebrate International
> Women's Day?" It was a great question; I didn't have a
> good response.

Learning about International Women's Day while living overseas was an awakening. Recognizing women's contributions beyond motherhood speaks to my soul. Motherhood is a large part of how I define myself but doesn't represent all of me. I am a better mother because I make an economic contribution to society. I am politically aware; I champion women's access to healthcare and education. I see myself as equal to men.

Nickie and I went to work recruiting a panel of women to cover the four core pillars of gender parity that the World Economic Forum measures and that the United Nations focuses on for International Women's Day. We leveraged the official UN theme, "Be Bold for Change," to create invitations, secure event space, get a deep discount on wine from a local vineyard, and then we headed to Costco for snacks. Eighty-four people showed up and stayed for over two hours of acknowledging women and building a community to accelerate gender parity. We were thrilled and patted ourselves on the back for a great job and moved on.

The following September, we started to receive emails from the International Women's Day Celebration attendees asking where the event was in 2017. The first event had made an impact. There was still so much work to be done on gender equity and so little awareness of IWD in Seattle; we agreed to host for a second year.

This time we enlisted the help of a notable local nonprofit to lend resources and event-planning expertise. A friend offered a space for

150 people; we were off and running. We again assembled a panel along with a few individual speakers to share their stories of "Being Bold" and working to overcome gender inequality. Responses topped 350 people, and we scrambled to find a bigger venue a few weeks before the event.

In the euphoria that followed our second IWD celebratory event, we formed our own nonprofit and agreed that the event would be bigger and better the following year. We put a deposit down on the Seattle Symphony Hall for March of 2018. The "Be Bold" nonprofit business license arrived in April 2017. In the last three years, the Be Bold IWD Celebration has drawn sellout crowds of over five hundred attendees.

The Next Unplanned Journey

People, men and women alike, have started to come forward to share their stories on the Be Bold Now platform about overcoming challenges and how they are working toward gender equality in all aspects of their lives. I wake up every day looking forward to hearing stories and connecting the community that has developed around the International Women's Day mission to recognize and celebrate women's contributions. I started writing about gender balance issues and speaking on podcasts, presenting to women's groups and to corporate audiences about being *bold*.

I still needed to earn a living, so diligently, I followed up on leads, spent time networking, refreshing my résumé, and interviewing to find a "real job."

I got a call from a headhunter who had seen my profile on LinkedIn and who was looking for a senior leader to partner with a

CEO of a Seattle-based mid-sized technology company. It was a tailor-made job for me. I breezed through two phone interviews and was invited to meet the CEO within a few days. I was happy and relieved. I was finally going to get a real job and could slide back into the mainstream of life. I would fit in again.

Ten minutes into the meeting with the CEO, it hit me. *This is a great job, nice guy, but I don't want to do this. I don't want to fit into a "normal" life.* I have never been successful following the typical path.

Every day, women tell me that they can't because they don't have the right education, the right connections, the right resources, or that they have responsibilities, a family, or have to consider their spouse's job or ego. My response is always, "Have you tried?"

I never imagined that my life would be the stories that fill these pages. I am opportunistic and never believe all of the reasons why not. I take chances, ask questions, and continue to pursue a career that offers an interesting life.

I started writing this book at the suggestion of a friend eight months ago. I never planned on writing a book, but it came quickly and has been cathartic. Putting my story on paper and gathering the nerve to share it has made me realize that I have always been happier and more successful when I am open to opportunities rather than planning my path.

My passion is to support women and to build a community of women and men that will fight for gender equity. This community I envision is one that brings a cultural change in how women are valued in business structures and within society as a whole. A community where women lift one another instead of competing with each other. A community where women can relate, celebrate, and champion each other's success. A society that isn't afraid to ask each other for help. The community I wish I had at my lowest points. Be Bold Now is that community.

Life is a series of twists and turns. My success has come through being open to the possibilities and seeking out situations and people that fill my soul. I have once again reinvented myself. This version of me includes being an author, a motivator, and a community builder.

I hope that this story provides examples of what is possible. I want women to relate to the feelings I have shared. But, more than anything, I want you, the reader, to feel inspired and empowered to explore your own path even when it changes course or is different than they thought it was going to be. I want you to join the community that believes in and is working toward gender equity. I want you to *be bold*.

about the author

Kate Isler is an activist, wife, author, mother, partner, friend, businessperson, sister, and risk-taker. Born in Southeast Texas, raised in the Southwest, and educated in the Northwest, Kate said "yes" to adventure and career from the start. As a tech executive, Kate's work took her all over the world with her husband as they raised three sons.

Kate started her career with Microsoft in Redmond, Washington. As a woman in tech in the early 1990s, Kate faced and overcame barriers in her work, and in the many countries where she lived, with humor and resilience. She was a trailblazer in her industry and in her personal life as she boldly stepped into the role as primary breadwinner, with the support of her husband, Doug.

After twenty years with Microsoft, Kate took her passion for business into the startup world. With her depth of experience in tech, this healthcare-focused app grew almost to fruition. Kate considers this one of her best experiences as she learned "what not to do." A shift into a non-profit startup dedicated to celebrating International Women's Day was the catalyst to Kate's most recent adventure, launching an ecommerce platform for women-owned businesses, TheWMarketplace. Kate's passion for gender parity has led her to a seat on the global board of Girl Rising, and she is a committed mentor for the International Women's Forum.

Kate lives in Seattle, Washington, with her husband. Their three sons are all grown and starting their own adventures.